CONTEMPORARY WRITERS

General Editors
MALCOLM BRADBURY
and
CHRISTOPHER BIGSBY

ALAIN ROBBE-GRILLET

ALAIN
ROBBE-GRILLET

JOHN FLETCHER

METHUEN
LONDON AND NEW YORK

First published in 1983 by
Methuen & Co. Ltd
11 New Fetter Lane, London EC4P 4EE
Published in the USA by
Methuen & Co.
in association with Methuen, Inc.
733 Third Avenue, New York, NY 10017

Typeset by Rowland Phototypesetting Ltd
Printed in Great Britain by
Richard Clay (The Chaucer Press) Ltd
Bungay, Suffolk

British Library Cataloguing in Publication Data

Fletcher, John, 19.. –
Alain Robbe-Grillet.—(Contemporary writers)
1. Robbe-Grillet, Alain—Criticism and
interpretation
I. Title   II. Series
843'.914   PQ2635.O/

ISBN   0–416–34420–8

Library of Congress Cataloging in Publication Data

Fletcher, John, 1937–
Alain Robbe-Grillet

(Contemporary writers)
Bibliography: p.
1. Robbe-Grillet, Alain, 1922–   --Criticism and
interpretation.   I. Title.   II. Series
PQ2635.0117Z63 1983   843'.914   83–13077
ISBN   0–416–34420–8 (pbk.)

For John Weightman,
with admiration and respect

CONTENTS

GENERAL EDITORS' PREFACE

The contemporary is a country which we all inhabit, but there is little agreement as to its boundaries or its shape. The serious writer is one of its most sensitive interpreters, but criticism is notoriously cautious in offering a response or making a judgement. Accordingly, this continuing series is an endeavour to look at some of the most important writers of our time, and the questions raised by their work. It is, in effect, an attempt to map the contemporary, to describe its aesthetic and moral topography.

The series came into existence out of two convictions. One was that, despite all the modern pressures on the writer and on literary culture, we live in a major creative time, as vigorous and alive in its distinctive way as any that went before. The other was that, though criticism itself tends to grow more theoretical and apparently indifferent to contemporary creation, there are grounds for a lively aesthetic debate. This series, which includes books written from various standpoints, is meant to provide a forum for that debate. By design, some of those who have contributed are themselves writers, willing to respond to their contemporaries; others are critics who have brought to the discussion of current writing the spirit of contemporary criticism or simply a conviction, forcibly and coherently argued, for the contemporary significance of their subjects. Our aim, as the series develops, is to continue to explore the works of major post-war writers – in fiction, drama and poetry – over an international range, and thereby to illuminate not only those works but also in some degree the artistic, social and moral assumptions on which they rest. Our wish is that, in their very variety of approach and emphasis, these books will stimulate interest in and understanding of the vitality of a living literature which, because it is contemporary, is especially ours.

Norwich, England   MALCOLM BRADBURY
                                                          CHRISTOPHER BIGSBY

PREFACE AND ACKNOWLEDGEMENTS

Alain Robbe-Grillet has usually been seen as an austere ex-perimentalist in the novel, addicted to arid, interminable de-scriptions of such unremarkable objects as coffee-pots, erasers and pieces of string. His own occasionally rather aggressive theoretical statements have been partly to blame for this unattractive image. It is, however, an image belied by the popular success of the film *Last Year at Marienbad* (directed by Alain Resnais to a script by Robbe-Grillet), and by the critical esteem in which novels like *The Voyeur* and *Jealousy* are held. This short study attempts to resolve the paradox by offering a new interpretation of Robbe-Grillet's work, one that stresses the subversive qualities of his imagination, and the disturbing power of his vision of a world of labyrinths and bizarre sexual stereotypes, haunted by images of love and loss.

Most critics start with a discussion of Robbe-Grillet's theory of the novel. I prefer to look at the novels first, and approach the theory through them. For that reason theoretical considera-tions are placed at the end of this book.

Since his collaboration with Resnais on *Marienbad* Robbe-Grillet has made a number of films himself. This is a book about the art of fiction, so the purely cinematic and cineastic dimensions of his work are left to specialists. But I do discuss those films for which a script – a 'cine-novel', to use his term – or a detailed synopsis has been published.

I should like to thank Roy Armes, Christopher Bigsby, Malcolm Bradbury, Ralph Yarrow and my wife, Beryl S. Fletcher, for valuable advice and help in the writing of this book. Once again, too, students at the University of East Anglia — especially those in my post-modernism seminar — have had much to contribute.

The author and publisher would like to thank the following for permission to reproduce copyright material: Calder & Boyars Ltd and Grove Press, Inc. for extracts from *Snapshots and Towards a New Novel*.

Norwich, England, 1983   JOHN FLETCHER

A NOTE ON THE TEXTS

Page references for quotations from Robbe-Grillet's works are to the British editions listed in the bibliography. Where the work has not been translated, reference is made to the original French publication. Wherever possible I have used existing translations, and in doing so I have carried out the occasional silent correction in order to make the wording more literal, or to bring it closer to the spirit of the French original; otherwise all translations are my own. Where a text has not been translated at the time of writing, I use the French title in order to avoid confusion later on. Where a translated title is available it is used throughout, and, in the few cases in which British and American titles differ, the former are employed.

The following abbreviations have been used:

Ob.   *Obliques*, 16–17 (1978)
STNN   *Snapshots and Towards a New Novel* (London: Calder & Boyars, 1965)

1

THRESHOLD AND LABYRINTH

> I write in order to destroy, by means of an exact description, nocturnal monsters which threaten my waking hours. (*Fragment autobiographique imaginaire*)

Whether we are happy about it or not, Alain Robbe-Grillet is firmly *out there*, France's most significant – though not necessarily greatest – living writer, a man who has changed the face of world literature for better or for worse. 'I live in the age of Alain Robbe-Grillet,' announces John Fowles's narrator in *The French Lieutenant's Woman*, and the mere mention of his name is sufficient to indicate that the book cannot be a novel in the traditionally received sense of the term.[1] Robbe-Grillet is an inescapable presence on the literary scene, a writer with whom one may violently disagree but whom one cannot ignore; a novelist who has made it difficult – if not impossible – to write serious fiction in the classic modes inherited from the nineteenth century, at any rate not without needing to justify (as Fowles does) a decision to retain at least some of the forms of the past.

The writer who has given so many people an uneasy literary conscience is one of the great prose stylists of the French language this century, and one of the most influential figures on the intellectual landscape in France since the heyday of Sartre and Camus in the 1940s. The ignominious military collapse of France in May 1940 deeply marked people of Robbe-Grillet's generation – he was nearly 18 at the time – and led them to question the very bases of Sartre's political commitment to radical politics and Camus's stoic retreat into a form of tragic humanism. Their own response was to cast doubt on entities like character and identity which their elders, however searching their political and moral inquiry, still took for granted. They perceived instability and relativity where Sartre and Camus assumed the ground to be firm, and translated their perceptions of immediacy into works of the imagination that are loosely defined as the *nouveau roman*. This term, which I shall return to in a moment, has achieved universal currency, the English equivalent 'new novel' not having caught on.

Although Sartre died only recently, in 1980, twenty years after Camus's death in a motor accident, he had been eclipsed as a living intellectual force for some time by a brash young man whose background was not literary or philosophical at all, but who had been trained in the applied sciences. Alain Robbe-Grillet even had an improbable name for a literary person; he was later felt to have made a pun on it in *Project for a Revolution in New York*, when he refers to a girl who burns a triangular hole in the pubic region of her dress. Critics were not slow to see this as 'à l'aine robe grillée' or 'dress charred in the groin'.[2] Intellectuals are not well known in France for a readiness to make fun of themselves, but in this, as in so much else, Robbe-Grillet is an exception.

Surprisingly for someone who still looks young, Robbe-Grillet is now over 60. He was born on 18 August 1922, the child of what he has called 'extreme right-wing anarchists'. He grew up mainly in Paris, but the Brittany of his birth and the high Jura region his father came from were parts of France he frequently visited as a boy. Memories of these places are imprinted on the fiction: *The Voyeur*, for instance, is set on an island off the Breton coast. The young Robbe-Grillet was sexually precocious, indulging in 'solitary pleasures which were already strongly marked by sadism'.[3] He was educated at *lycées* in Paris and Brest and at the Institut National Agronomique; he passed the *agrégation d'agronomie* in 1945, then went overseas to conduct biological research, but was repatriated in 1951 for health reasons. In 1955 he became literary adviser at the Editions de Minuit – a post he still holds – where he has had particular responsibility for the fiction list. In 1957 he married Catherine Rstakian; they have no children. Catherine Robbe-

Grillet is of more than incidental interest: she may well have written a pornographic novel called *L'Image* (1956) which reads as if it were inspired by Robbe-Grillet, and she has acted in secondary parts in some of his films. In French women's magazines and in Paris gossip generally, they are reputed to be a very close but sexually unconventional couple.

Robbe-Grillet is, however, a very private person, and not much is known about his life. He did spend some time in Nuremberg under the German forced labour scheme during the war, but he has said little about this beyond the fact that the factory which is the setting of his first novel may be identified with the one he worked in. His literary beginnings were modest: a few early poems have been published in the Robbe-Grillet special number of the review *Obliques*; so too has a text of 1947 describing a young people's visit to Bulgaria. He is a slow and meticulous worker, and his total output is not large. In any case, as a research scientist he did not at first have much time for writing. Nevertheless he did finish his first novel in 1949; it was, however, rejected by the leading Paris publishers and published only in 1978. Entitled *Un Régicide*, it is a novel of anxiety and enigma, of humour tinged with fear as in Hitchcock, where terror is undermined by laughter, the comic dimension of mystery. It is 'about' the murder of a king (hence the title) which does not come off – indeed, seems to have been purely a figment of the hero's imagination – and it has so much in common with later works that, if one did not know it had genuinely existed since 1949, one would be tempted to think that Robbe-Grillet created it much later in a riot of self-pastiche.

In this book there is a 'last year' as in *Marienbad*, a large black dog as in *The Immortal One*, an island as in *The Voyeur*, repulsive insects as in *Jealousy*, a destroyed town as in *Topology of a Phantom City*, and fear of being cut off by the rising tide as in *Snapshots*. Its early composition is, however, betrayed by its derivativeness: it owes a lot to surrealism – to which the scale of Robbe-Grillet's debt is clearer now than would have been the case in 1949 if it had been published then

– and it is also influenced by the authors Robbe-Grillet read at the time, an unlikely combination of Graham Greene, James Cain, Franz Kafka and Raymond Roussel. Robbe-Grillet is unconventional even in his reading, believing that it is not, as Malraux thought, familiarity with great works which alone encourages one to write, but that quite minor books can stimulate creativity. Thus the influence on *The Erasers* of Graham Greene, whom Robbe-Grillet considers only a second-rate author, exists side by side with an admiration for the very highbrow novelist Maurice Blanchot, whom most people in the English-speaking world have probably heard of only as a literary critic.

As important to Robbe-Grillet as what he read was his encounter with experimental science. His specialism was research into diseases affecting such tropical fruits as the banana (*Jealousy* is set in a banana plantation, and he lived for a time in the sort of spacious colonial house that is minutely described in the book). For him, science is not so far removed from literature as proponents of the 'two cultures' would have us believe. Thus, characteristically, he observed in 1975 that 'science does not aim to cover exhaustively the whole of reality, but to construct systems and concepts which will perhaps – and it is a big perhaps – allow man to act on the world.'[4] In like manner he suggested that 'mineralogy, botany and zoology seek knowledge of textures (both internal and external), of their organization, functioning and genesis', the implication of this remark, in *Towards a New Novel* (*STNN*, p. 92), being that literature, or any other art form, is wasting its time if it attempts to penetrate the essence of things. It is undoubtedly his scientific background which inspires Robbe-Grillet to make such trenchant assertions.

His scientific career is now at an end, however, and literature – evidently always his deepest passion – is now his livelihood. But he is and always has been a poet, not much in verse, but a great deal in prose of this measured and elegiac kind:

It speaks of calm, fertile valleys and of village festivals: after a day spent in the grape harvest the new wine is drunk straight from the press, and then as the sun sets you fall drunkenly asleep with the washer-women, encircled in their white arms. (*Un Régicide*, p. 117)

In spite of considerable notoriety – and respectable sales around the world, with as many as 40 per cent of his works in French being sold outside France – Robbe-Grillet is hardly a popular writer, and he claims that no one has ever really understood what it is he is trying to achieve. There is some truth in this. As recently as 1971, in fact, Roger Poole could write that he 'despises humanism' and prides himself on 'rising above the weakness of human nature',[5] whereas the facts are that he goes to great lengths in *Towards a New Novel* and elsewhere to make clear that, far from setting himself above other people, he has all the normal emotions and weaknesses – and that the only humanism he feels contempt for is the facile anthropocentric fallacy of nineteenth-century positivism, and the reaction to it in the guise of Camus's tragic pessimism. Since he has no religious belief, he would even claim, somewhat indignantly, that in his world humanity is on the contrary supreme, because it is alone, subordinated to no one and nothing in the universe.

The blurb on a 1962 mass-market reprint of Robbe-Grillet's first published novel made the following comment:

The 'new novel', which has deeply marked literature of the up-and-coming variety, recognizes in Alain Robbe-Grillet its theorist and trail-blazer. This new vision of people and of the world finds in Robbe-Grillet's novel its most striking exemplar.

That statement is typical of many that have been made, not only in France but throughout the world, since *The Erasers* was published in 1953, but like other journalistic statements it oversimplifies what have been complex and even contradictory elements in the novels' reception. There are in fact almost as many Robbe-Grillets as there are critics of his work. Early French reactions were predictably hostile and uncomprehending – the equivalent, on the literary level, of the 'pot of paint flung in the public's face' sort of criticism – but these soon gave way, in serious organs of opinion, to more thoughtful responses. In 1954 the then relatively little-known Roland Barthes published a highly influential essay on *The Erasers*, and on one or two of the short texts later collected under the title *Snapshots*. This offered a philosophical interpretation which stressed the epistemological questioning at the heart of Robbe-Grillet's enterprise and projected him as a *chosiste*, the founder of an *école du regard*, which has remained for many the standard image of this writer. A decade later, in his seminal book *Les Romans de Robbe-Grillet* (1963), Bruce Morrissette moved away from Barthes's phenomenological stance almost to the other extreme, and adopted a psychological approach which stressed the subjectivity, accurately recorded, of the total vision of Robbe-Grillet's fictional world, and the obsessive quality of his narrators.

Younger critics such as Stephen Heath later drew attention to the possibility of a linguistics-based criticism which stressed the novelist as user of language in a world in which language *is* reality, not merely its vehicle or what encodes it. Heath's book, *The Nouveau Roman: A Study in the Practice of Writing* (1972), was a development of the work of Roland Barthes in *S/Z* and in other explorations of the theory of fiction. A more narrowly linguistic line was meanwhile being pursued in France by the critic and novelist Jean Ricardou, and his writings, especially *Pour une théorie du nouveau roman* (1971), have been interpreted, adapted and humanized for English-speaking readers by Ann Jefferson in her monograph *The Nouveau Roman and the Poetics of Fiction* (1980). This argues that language creates ambiguity and paranoia in Robbe-Grillet's teleological structures; our view of history, Jefferson concludes, is 'coloured by our view of the language through which it is constructed, and our view of that language is equally determined by the kind of history which it elaborates.'[6]

In so energetically precipitating definitions in this way, Robbe-Grillet's novels reveal their strangeness (as well, paradoxically, as their richness, at first glance an unlikely word to apply to writing of this kind); but they also raise the suspicion that sophisticated approaches like these not only feed off but also in their own way provoke the sort of text Robbe-Grillet has been writing recently. In these later works, based on *mise-en-abyme* – a technical term which covers infinite regression, reflexivity and self-quotation, and is perhaps most simply exemplified by the play-within-the-play in *Hamlet* – the influences of other French critics and theorists can be discerned in a manner often to the detriment of the interest and originality of Robbe-Grillet's writing itself. The close relationship between Jean Ricardou and Robbe-Grillet seems particularly incestuous in this respect. Ricardou – who was a member for a time of the famous group of intellectuals led by Philippe Sollers, closely associated with the avant-garde journal *Tel Quel* – is at once a formidable theorist, an interesting critic and a novelist of small talent. Only the genius of Claude Simon (a *nouveau romancier* who is Robbe-Grillet's senior by some nine years) has been able to withstand the onslaught of this devastating combination, which has the same effect on literary fertility as the arrival of a particularly hungry swarm of locusts on a field of ripe corn. Robbe-Grillet, perhaps because he is not such a singleminded and obstinately self-obsessed creator as Simon, sometimes gives the impression of having been stripped bare by the locusts.

Whatever reservations one has about some of Robbe-Grillet's friends and fellow theorists, though, they have the merit of proclaiming unambiguously the revolutionary importance of his writing. The time has now come, perhaps – it is after all over thirty years since his first book appeared – for a closer look at their claim, not with an iconoclastic and quite misplaced urge to dismiss his significance, but to take advantage of the perspective an interval of three decades or more gives us to take stock of the real achievement of a writer whose name is synonymous, wherever contemporary literature is discussed, with a radically new approach not merely to the writing of fiction but to an understanding of the world. The present study might be subtitled 'How to Stop Being Frightened of the *Nouveau Roman* and to Begin Liking Robbe-Grillet'. My approach is different from that of previous critics – the most important of whose works are listed in the bibliography – because I look at the total impact of the writing and not just at its language, its treatment of objects, or its departures from conventional narrative. I do not always follow Robbe-Grillet's own assertions of intent; but then does he not say himself that one of his diatribes against metaphor is exactly contemporaneous with *Jealousy*, which 'from its title to the least of its insects is a huge snare of metaphorical readings' (*Ob*., p. 2)?

Robbe-Grillet is an ironist and a joker who 'pinches without a smile', as the French say, so the reader is even more justified than usual in not accepting the writer's account of his intentions as being all there is to be said. Indeed, if we take too seriously some utterances of the polemical Robbe-Grillet, and even more those of his acolytes like Jean Ricardou, we end in an impasse. He becomes a writer's writer of the most rarefied kind, an experimental, 'laboratory' novelist whose appeal to a wide circle of readers around the world becomes a mystery. As I indicated, a large proportion of his French-language books are exported; he has been translated into every major world language; he is an essential point of reference wherever contemporary literature is mentioned or discussed. To have had such an impact, to dominate the literary scene at home and abroad in this way, can be explained only by an appeal to the reader which goes beyond, and cannot be illuminated by, the rather sterile elucubrations of the ruling politburo of literary criticism in Paris at the moment. So my own aim is the humbler, less glamorous but more necessary one of reading the novels as 'straight' as possible, without preconceptions based either on tradition – those Robbe-Grillet warns so pertinently against in *Towards a New Novel* – or on an over-academic reaction to that traditional mode of reading as being too 'unsophisticated'.

I shall not have much to say about the *nouveau roman* as such. It is not best seen as evidence of a 'movement', still less a 'school'. Indeed, I have never been impressed by attempts to show that this very disparate group of novelists, who came to prominence in France after 1950, have more than a few basic ideas about fiction and reality in common. There is no such thing, to my mind, as an 'aesthetic' of the new novel – simply a few points about the necessity of a new approach to plot and character which seem to be shared by most of them. Besides, it is now over thirty years since the *nouveau roman* emerged, and its other major figures – Claude Simon, Nathalie Sarraute, Robert Pinget and Michel Butor – have gone on publishing actively ever since, and in many cases have taken a path radically different from Robbe-Grillet's. In any case he too has altered: I shall be arguing that there is a perceptible change in his style and subject-matter from the mid-sixties onwards. Even so he, like the others, shows remarkable consistency, not to say stamina, over the years. Once we have accustomed ourselves to what is inevitably at first an unfamiliar narrative manner, we find that his novels can exert a great fascination and can even be quite spine-chilling at times. What is more, in spite of his often bellicose attacks on 'tragic' humanism, it is clear that he too is concerned with the basic facts of the human condition and of our situation in the world; it is just that he sees them differently and so wishes his readers to confront them afresh and through his eyes, rather than through those of writers who, he claims, have not accepted that since the time of Balzac everything in our world has changed.

Much the same is true of film and the new cinema which arose alongside, and in some ways in parallel with, the *nouveau roman*. It was to be expected that a visual novelist like Robbe-Grillet, for whom the eye is an instrument, and the act of perception a form of research, should turn to the cinema as soon as he could find backers for his productions. In his perceptually oriented world the slatted screens of the novel *Jealousy* convert effortlessly into the Turkish blinds of the film *The Immortal One*. More recently, but just as predictably, Robbe-Grillet has turned to painting as a form of expression; his works in this medium are abstracts, consisting for the most part of newsprint on which red paint is splashed, but he also paints the naked bodies of the actresses who perform in his films and in turn gets them to imprint their shapes on white surfaces. A particularly Robbe-Grilletian form of *Gesamt-kunstwerk*? Perhaps so; what is certainly true is that the visual arts are central to his preoccupations.

2

ANXIETY AND ENIGMA

He was too tired to survey all the conclusions arising from the story, and the trains of thought into which it was leading him were unfamiliar, dealing with impalpabilities better suited to a theme for discussion among court officials than for him. The simple story had lost its clear outline . . . (Franz Kafka, *The Trial*)

In some ways Robbe-Grillet has more in common with painters than he has with novelists, at least with writers of a 'highbrow' kind (I shall come to the other sort, Raymond Chandler and John le Carré, in a moment). One of the great modern artists who haunt him is Paul Delvaux; it is not surprising to find that they collaborated on a limited-edition art book, *Construction d'un temple en ruines à la déesse Vanadé*, with etchings by Delvaux and text by Robbe-Grillet, in 1975. Delvaux's masterpiece of 1941, *La Ville inquiète* ('The Anxious Town'), projects an image of melancholy, disquiet and bafflement that is particularly close to the atmosphere of Robbe-Grillet's early fiction. This dense composition features bare-breasted, middle-aged women looking startled as a hesitant, bespectacled old man, dressed like a 1920s solicitor in dark suit, wing collar and bowler hat, gropes his way through a scene of confusion in a landscape of naked people and classical temples. A catastrophe seems to be impending, but these people are too paralysed by anxiety and doubt to do much about it. This theme is taken up by Robbe-Grillet in *Topology of a Phantom City*, the novel which includes the text that Delvaux illustrated. Clearly, the world of Delvaux and of other surrealist painters is one that has greatly shaped Robbe-Grillet's own ways of seeing, as is borne out by shots of people standing about motionless in sunlit, vacant spaces in *Marienbad* and *The Immortal One*. Turbid eroticism, too; expressed in a crystalline sharpness of perception, it is characteristic of both Robbe-Grillet and Delvaux.

This is especially true of the novels of the 1950s, written in a prose style which is at once transparent and opaque, something Beckett is describing when he alludes (in *Watt*, published by coincidence in the same year as *The Erasers* but written a decade before) to a discourse 'of great formal brilliance and indeterminable purport'.[7] The formal brilliance arises from an exact process of discrimination and from the close relation of subject and predicate in the sentence, as in this characteristic example from *The Voyeur*:

> A rectangular shadow less than a foot wide crossed the white dust of the road. It lay at a slight angle from the perpendicular without quite reaching the opposite side: its rounded – almost flat – extremity did not protrude beyond the middle of the road, of which the left side remained unshaded. (p. 75)

The indeterminable purport – the application of intelligence subsequent to action, and of comprehension through perception – relies on close-function shots in which gesture, not meaning, is dominant, as in the passage about the squashed frog which immediately follows the sentences just quoted:

> Between this extremity and the close-cropped weeds bordering the road had been crushed the corpse of a little frog, its legs open, its arms crossed, forming a slightly darker grey spot on the dust of the road. The creature's body had lost all thickness, as if nothing but the skin were left – hard, desiccated, and henceforth invulnerable – clinging to the ground as closely as the shadow of an animal about to leap, limbs extended – but somehow immobilized in air. (p. 75)

Because Robbe-Grillet came from an eminently 'highbrow' publisher, Jérôme Lindon's Editions de Minuit, critics at first thought this writing was without precedent, except possibly in Kafka's lucid visions of nightmare. But the following words, not written about Robbe-Grillet at all, neatly fit his case:

24

They are carefully structured enigmas. Incomplete disclosures and delayed resolutions move the reader backwards and forwards. . . . [The hero] remains ultimately unknowable and contradictory. . . . Again and again, we see how others react to [him], and sometimes his own reaction, but the meaning is always left for us to work on.[8]

This was said not of *The Erasers* or *The Voyeur* but of John le Carré's immensely popular book *Smiley's People*. Le Carré has made something of a speciality of enigmatic stories in which the systematic assemblage of the plot is more important than the subject-matter. Indeed, it becomes an end in itself, and as such can sometimes get out of hand. Derek Robinson has pointed out that not infrequently the plots of John le Carré, Len Deighton and other popular writers are inconsistent or otherwise flawed in a way which damages their plausibility, and that the conscientious reader can expect little help from either author or publisher when these lapses are pointed out to them. In popular fiction it matters, of course, if a story will not stand up to serious scrutiny. Alfred Hitchcock called films which are defective in this respect 'ice-box movies': their effectiveness, he claimed, lasted only until the spectator got home, opened his refrigerator for a beer, and then paused to utter the fateful words, 'Hey, wait a minute . . .', bringing the film's flimsy construction tumbling down. With Hitchcock it was a point of honour to make his own plots watertight.[9]

What Robbe-Grillet has done – especially in *The House of Assignation* and subsequent novels and films – is to exploit the 'ice-box' factor to the full, and produce plots which have inconsistencies and non sequiturs deliberately built into them, so that his 'carefully structured enigmas' are doubly enigmatic. Or, if you like, no longer enigmatic at all, since any work with an inherent self-destructing capability will no longer puzzle the reader but more likely amuse and impress him by its feeding – parasite-like, as so many post-modern creations do – on a degenerated archetype, transforming its decay into a new if somewhat fetid brilliance.

This was, however, a later development in Robbe-Grillet's career, and I shall return to the subject in Chapter 4. In his early works he was still developing stereotypes of popular fiction, not deconstructing them. *The Erasers*, in particular, is an act of homage to the art of such masters of the medium as Raymond Chandler. 'The French are the only people I know', Chandler once said, 'who think about writing as writing', adding: 'it doesn't matter a damn what a novel is about . . . the only fiction of any moment in any age is that which does magic with words.'[10] The French have returned the compliment by discerning a *rhétorique de la nostalgie* in Chandler's fiction.[11] Perhaps the greatest French tribute to the Anglo-Saxon espionage or mystery story, though, is the fiction I discuss in this chapter.

The Erasers (*Les Gommes*), Robbe-Grillet's second novel and his first published, appeared in 1953. Put succinctly, its subject is 'vingt-quatre heures en trop', the 'superfluous' day during which the action takes place. Robbe-Grillet has himself described the novel as a detective story, with a murderer, a sleuth and a corpse, and the traditional functions are respected in that the murderer fires the fatal shot, the victim dies, and the detective solves the mystery for everyone's benefit. But the relationship between these functions is less straightforward than is usually the case, or at least it becomes straightforward only at the end.

> For the novel is precisely the account of the twenty-four hours which run from the moment of the shot being fired to that of the victim's death, the time the bullet takes to travel a dozen or so feet: twenty-four 'superfluous' hours.[12]

The novel opens in a café, where the proprietor is mechanically preparing for the day and meditating on the death the previous evening of a neighbour, Daniel Dupont. He goes to awake a client in the only bedroom he has to let, but the man has already left. Downstairs somebody (Garinati) asks after the client, whose name is Wallas. Garinati, acting on orders from

Bona to assassinate Dupont, had hidden the previous evening in Dupont's study. He fired one shot at Dupont as the latter entered his study after dinner, but missed, wounding his victim only slightly. The morning papers, however, carry the news that Dupont died from several shots. This is a story put about officially in order to mislead the assassins; in reality Dupont is hiding in the clinic of a doctor friend and will be driven secretly to Paris later in the day. The gang who tried to kill him are expected to strike again at another target, and the government are anxious that Dupont's lucky escape should remain a secret from them.

Wallas, a special agent, has been sent from the capital to investigate the murder. His watch has stopped; indeed, by coincidence it stopped at 7.30 the previous evening at the moment when Dupont 'died'. He arrived late the night before in this provincial town, which he hardly knows, having visited it only once as a child. One of his first actions on his first day in the place is to buy an eraser. He also calls on the local police chief with whom he is to collaborate in the investigation, only to find that the matter has been taken out of the inspector's hands (naturally, because the authorities in Paris do not wish the fact that no murder has taken place to become public). In their conversation it transpires that Wallas's revolver – which happens to be the same calibre as the one fired at Dupont – has one cartridge missing from the magazine.

Wallas begins his investigation. He learns that a man, who bears a close resemblance to Wallas himself, interfered with Dupont's electric doorbell prior to the murder. When he goes to the local post office he is mistaken for someone else and given mail addressed to a Mr André VS (Wallas is pronounced 'Vallas' in French). Then Wallas remembers that he came to the town as a child with his mother, and that the purpose of the trip was to see his father, from whom his mother was separated. Wallas's information leads him to hide in Dupont's study later that evening, but the man who enters the study is not one of the assassination squad: it is Dupont himself who has returned for some important papers. Seeing Wallas, whom he does not know, he aims his revolver at him, but the special agent – who thinks this is Dupont's assassin – fires first and kills Dupont. It is 7.30; the failed act has gone back to its starting-point for a second try. Wallas's watch starts ticking again, exactly twenty-four hours after it stopped.

The parallels between this detective story and the myth of Oedipus are now obvious (though they were not at the time, Samuel Beckett apparently being the first of Robbe-Grillet's readers to notice the allusion); it soon becomes clear that Wallas is Dupont's son and that in killing his own father he is fulfilling his destiny. The erasers which Wallas buys during the day are the focus for projected oedipal erotic sensations (oedipal because the manufacturer's trademark is 'Œdipe', erotic because Wallas enjoys the tactile sensation of soft rubber on his fingers), but they have no significance in themselves and certainly do not offer any key to the meaning of the novel. This is provided by the structure of classical tragedy – a prologue, five chapters and an epilogue – and by the circular nature of the story, which begins and ends in the café where Wallas has taken a room. The pastiche of mystery stories is overt and effective: various red herrings are dragged across the path, and a strong feeling of suspense develops towards the end, making the novel as exciting to read as the books it elaborately imitates, and it reminds one of Hitchcock too in its theme of guilt by association. But the espionage genre is another that is alluded to; the assassins are an anarchist group and have already committed nine murders of a similar nature, all of men holding important semi-official political positions: Dupont, for instance, is an economics professor.

The Erasers is an impressively skilful work of intricate coincidences and character interrelationships, in which the narrative's own discourse on itself becomes quite audible.[13] Robbe-Grillet's ingenuity has been rewarded by the highest sale in France of any of his books; but, though it is entertaining, it is not without its faults. It may avoid Chandler's mawkishness, snobbery and coy metaphors, but Robbe-Grillet is too high-handed in his construction and too ready to mystify. He wants to have his cake and eat it: he imitates popular genres but does not need to stick to their rules. He can and does leave some loose ends – such as how or why Wallas came to be mistaken for someone else at the poste restante – whereas a writer like Chandler would avoid them. So although *The Erasers* was to prove one of Robbe-Grillet's most 'acceptable' books it is scarcely his most characteristic. Indeed, now that his first novel, *Un Régicide*, has finally been published, we can see that *The Erasers* was the nearest this inescapably esoteric writer could come to producing a book that would readily find an audience. By the same token, however, *The Erasers* is less centrally and urgently an expression of Robbe-Grillet's vision than either *Un Régicide* or his third novel (but second published), *The Voyeur*.

Around the time *The Voyeur* appeared, in the mid-fifties, he was publishing a number of shorter prose texts which were later collected under the title *Snapshots* (*Instantanés*, 1962). These share a sense of unease – even of ill-contained hysteria – masked by meticulous description. Two of them are about the menacing power of the sea and the danger of being cut off by the rising tide, and in an autobiographical fragment Robbe-Grillet has revealed that as a child he was terrified of the ocean close to which he was born. I have already mentioned that *The Voyeur* is set in the same sort of landscape as that of the Brest region in which he spent part of every year as a child; in *Snapshots*, too, the sea is sinister and unfriendly. But not all the *Snapshots* are about fear of water; there is a famous one about a coffee-pot on a table, and if one believed some of Robbe-Grillet's early critics one would be forgiven for thinking that he never wrote about anything else. In fact, that particular text is called 'The Dress-maker's Dummy' and is as much a description of reflections and distortions within a well-lit room as a meditation on a coffee-pot, and it ends with the rather disturbing information that the design of the tile on which the coffee-pot stands 'represents an owl, with two big, somewhat terrifying eyes' (*STNN*, p. 5) which fortunately cannot 'for the moment' be seen, since the tile serves as a mat for the hot pot of coffee. What is more, dressmakers' dummies emerge in Robbe-Grillet's colour films of the 1970s as obsessive erotic clichés.

Later critics, less mesmerized by *chosisme*, recognized that the *Snapshots* were entirely characteristic compositions, almost Robbe-Grillet novels in miniature, or fragments of larger works never completed. Indeed, they bear a similar relation to the full-length works as Kafka's short stories do to his novels: they contain much of the artist's world in condensed form. They presumably also served as practice pieces like five-finger exercises for the composition of *The Voyeur* and *In the Labyrinth*, to which they are closely related both structurally and thematically; all of them, that is, except the last one, 'The Secret Room', which was written specially for the collection of *Snapshots* published in volume form in 1962, and has more in common with the works I shall be discussing in Chapter 4.

It therefore serves as a useful introduction to *The Voyeur* to read some of the *Snapshots* first, especially 'The Way Back' and 'The Beach', which have the same setting as the novel. *The Voyeur* (*Le Voyeur*, 1955) could equally well have been called 'Le Voyageur', since the hero, Mathias, is a travelling watch salesman who is visiting the island of his birth on a day trip. He needs several good sales in order to restore his shaky finances and thinks the place where he once lived should provide good territory for that purpose. Soon after his arrival he hears of a 13-year-old girl, Jacqueline Leduc, who despite her youth already has a dubious reputation. While trying to sell a watch to the girl's mother, Mathias sees a photograph of Jacqueline which reminds him of another girl he once knew and evidently was emotionally involved with, Violette, and in thinking of Jacqueline after that he will tend to apply to her the name of Violette. The girl disappears during the course of the day. Mathias is delayed getting back to the ferry and just misses it. He has therefore to spend a few more days on the island. The next day Jacqueline's body is washed up, and everyone assumes that she died accidentally while playing on the cliffs. Mathias eventually leaves the island by the next boat.

30

It is clear, even from this brief outline of the story, that something is left out. Like Faulkner's novel *Sanctuary*, which greatly influenced writers in France after it was translated in the early thirties, *The Voyeur* is a *récit lacunaire* in which the centre is missing and has to be guessed at on the basis of indications left in the text when a hole was, as it were, burnt out of it. Clearly something took place between Mathias and Jacqueline which greatly disturbed Mathias afterwards; after he has missed the ferry – itself an act which was obviously unconsciously willed by him – he returns obsessively to the place where she was last seen alive (in order to remove clues he is aware of having left). There even seems to have been a witness to everything that happened before Jacqueline fell, or was thrown, off the cliff. This witness – the voyeur of the title – is Julien Marek, but he does not incriminate Mathias because he has his own reasons for wanting the girl dead. Mathias is therefore not suspected and is, to his surprise and relief, allowed to leave the island unmolested.

It is, of course, easy to reconstruct the methodical and sadistic rape and murder of Jacqueline by Mathias watched by Julien's terrible and accusing eyes, not only from the many indications in the text such as the splayed body of a frog that Mathias finds squashed on the road, but also from the pun on the name Violette (*viol* means rape in French); to do so, however, would be beside the point. As Robbe-Grillet himself points out, the gap in the text has an important organizational function in the novel: 'not only is the story centred round this blank spot, but it is this absence itself which presides over the writing of the entire book; it is a truly structural void, the void as a generator of the text' (*Ob.*, p. 62). The point of the book would be quite lost if the crime were to be described or shown. But, since what happened can easily be imagined by the reader, the novel is more than just an ingenious mystery story like *The Erasers*. Whereas *The Erasers* is a clever literary puzzle, fundamentally no more serious than the genre it pastiches, *The Voyeur* is a deeply disturbing book about real anxiety and obsessive, guilty fascination with evil. It is also more convinc-

31

ing on the purely realistic level: the island is a plausible setting for such a horrifying assault, and the uneasy conversations which Mathias conducts with various islanders he meets in the course of his sales drive are natural and unforced on their part. This is a significant point, since the reader must be made aware of how close Mathias often is to incriminating himself, but the people whom he accosts should not be.

In 1976 Robbe-Grillet published a film project entitled *Piège à fourrure* which has similarities with both of his first two novels. Like *The Erasers* it is about an investigation agent assigned an important mission which requires all his energies, but otherwise the story is similar to that of *The Voyeur*:

> As soon as he begins the job a very minor accident deflects the investigator from his path, purely temporarily, or so he thinks. For reasons at first moral, then sentimental or erotic, he finds himself drawn gradually into another affair, which seems to him to prey upon the one he is engaged in, since it causes dangerous hiccups in the execution of his duties. . . . But in the end what he tried to dismiss as a merely fortuitous upset turns out to be the very purpose of his mission.[14]

The same could be said of Mathias: he comes to the island to sell watches, but he ends up committing rape and murder, which perhaps in an obscure way was his unconscious intention all the time. Indeed, despite Robbe-Grillet's avowed aim of avoiding traditional psychology, his insight into the criminal mind — as his insight into the jealous mind in *Jealousy* — is fairly remarkable. Mathias betrays his mental disturbance by anxiously repeating phrases to himself like a needle stuck in a groove, and by what can only be called obsessive mental arithmetic as he calculates such things as how many watches he can sell by the hour.

Together with *In the Labyrinth*, this novel is the most Kafkaesque of Robbe-Grillet's books, the most redolent of Kafka's world of 'dark hallways lined with closed doors' (p. 58). The names (like Marek, or like Janeck in *The Erasers*) have a mid-European ring about them; a character (Jean Robin) is said to be long dead at one point in the story and yet his name is seen by Mathias written, evidently recently, in chalk on the door of a fisherman's cottage; and the confusion and lassitude that Mathias frequently experiences result from his being unable to find anything to cling to in his distress, 'any rule he could interpret as applicable – which might serve as an example for his conduct – behind which he could have entrenched himself' (p. 121). It is true that his condition has a factual basis in the migraine which afflicts him and which grows steadily more distracting, but the pain behind his eyes only serves to reinforce a sense of alienation and estrangement which seems inseparable from his condition. He is a man haunted by erotic obsessions – as Robbe-Grillet has pointed out, the text conceals a number of examples of triangles and other structures suggesting the outline of the female pubis – and lives in terror of labyrinths:

> Unfortunately none of the numerous existing paths coincided with the theoretical direction Mathias had selected; he was therefore confined, from the start, to one of two possible detours. Besides, every path looked winding and discontinuous – separating, reuniting, constantly interlacing, even stopping short in a briar patch. All of which obliged him to make many false starts, hesitations, retreats, posed new problems at every step, forbade any assurance as to the general direction of the path he had chosen. (p. 159)

This sort of anxiety gives *The Voyeur* much of its tense hold on the reader, but it is also gripping in a more traditional sense: there is straightforward suspense when Mathias is hurrying to catch the boat which will carry him away from his freshly committed crime, and considerable tension when he just misses it, and another and more Hitchcockian kind of terror when he realizes that young Marek has witnessed everything:

> Suddenly a wave of terror broke over Mathias: Julien . . . had taken cover and had watched. . . . There would have to be something more than suspicions – even detailed suspi-

cions – to justify the boy's assurance. Julien had 'seen'. There was no use denying it any longer. Only the images registered by those eyes could have given them that indelible, intolerable fixity. And yet they were quite ordinary grey eyes ... two perfect, motionless circles set side by side, each one pierced at the centre by a black hole. (pp. 182–3)

Into that abyss – the black hole at the centre of the eye of the 'voyeur' – Mathias's crime has been engulfed, as at the level of the text it has been swallowed up by the staring gap in the narrative. The sense of terror and guilt which this inspires reminds one, as I have said, of Hitchcock at his most remorseless. And yet, like Hitchcock's spine-chilling explorations of guilt, *The Voyeur* has its own kind of playfulness as the narrator shares with the reader a wry amusement at Mathias's largely unsuccessful attempts to fast-talk his way to easy sales with the canny fisher-folk, or at the appropriateness of the title of the film showing at the island's cinema: 'Mr X on the Double Circuit'. Indeed, it is itself doubly appropriate, because Mathias covers the same ground twice, and because of the ubiquitousness in the novel of the figure-of-eight motif, which represents among other things the two juxtaposed circles of the voyeur's eyes.

The text is rich in resonances of this kind. Just as *The Erasers* is based on a 'superfluous' twenty-four hours, Mathias loses about one hour of 'abnormal, excessive, suspicious, inexplicable time' (p. 173), the interval during which Jacqueline was murdered. Or was she? The salesman indulges in manic attempts to account for the use of his time – obviously as if it were as precious a commodity as the watches out of which he is trying to make a livelihood – because he is torn between two contrary impulses, the ego of his professional obligations and the id of his sexual fantasies. There appears to be a natural build-up to a criminal act through erotic obsessions, but the murder – if that is what it is – also arises intertextually, growing out of the account of a similar crime which was recently reported in a local newspaper and which Mathias has cut out

34

and kept guiltily in his wallet. (A similar form of *mise-en-abyme* is the so-called 'African novel' in *Jealousy*.) Another literary provocation is the local legend according to which 'each spring, a young virgin had to be hurled from the top of the cliff to appease the storm-god and render the sea kind to *travellers* and sailors' (p. 189; my italics). All the reader knows for sure is that there is a body, but the death *could* have been an accident, and indeed that is what the local fishermen assume. They must be experienced in finding corpses that have been attacked by sea creatures, sufficiently at least to tell the difference between cigarette burns and natural abrasions. If Mathias did not kill his 'Violette', he would have had no difficulty fantasizing the whole business, and then he might have felt intensely guilty about his fantasy. A man who can see in a simple snapshot of Jacqueline 'an ambiguous mixture of surrender and constraint' (p. 68) could certainly have embroidered richly upon the image. On the other hand, without the hypothesis of murder it is difficult to account for the role in the story of Julien, who – if Mathias is a rapist – becomes a true voyeur, because he has positively enjoyed watching Mathias act out his own obsessions for him.

The Voyeur is in my view Robbe-Grillet's finest work, a satisfying and moving piece of fiction in which the technique of narration is exactly appropriate to the subject, a novel which owes something of its form, manner and tone to the detective story – as Faulkner's *Sanctuary* also does – but which transcends its model. I am particularly impressed that Robbe-Grillet was able to handle an emotive topic – again, like Faulkner – without sensationalizing (or, worse, trivializing) it. This is all the more commendable as in later works – mainly those I shall discuss in Chapter 4 – he sometimes indulges in facile, even frivolous attitudes to sexual sadism. In *The Voyeur* he handles Jacqueline's rape with black humour, perhaps, but in such a way that the basic seriousness of Mathias's sick condition is not ignored or sidestepped. Like Hitchcock's late masterpiece *Frenzy*, it deals with what is after all a grave matter – the impulse to inflict hurt and damage on what one cannot ever truly possess – without either prurience or a misplaced permissiveness. This is not the case, unfortunately, with some of Robbe-Grillet's later novels and films.

After the disturbing eroticism of *The Voyeur* Robbe-Grillet turned to something more epistemologically unsettling in his next novel but one. *In the Labyrinth* (*Dans le labyrinthe*) was published in 1959, two years after *Jealousy* (which I shall come to in the next chapter). Superbly translated by Christine Brooke-Rose, *In the Labyrinth* deserves to be better known in the English-speaking world. Its method, as John Spurling noted on publication, is

> a series of images superimposed on one another, coalescing, separating, returning, [which] derives partly from Kafka. That is to say, although every detail is drawn with painstaking clarity, the elisional system of dovetailing and the subtle changes of tense give an overall impression of confusion, exactly as in dream or memory.[15]

This makes it a difficult book to summarize, but the basic story is of a soldier wandering around a large town in the depths of winter after a major military disaster, in search of a man to whom he needs to give a parcel containing the personal belongings of a dead comrade. The soldier is wounded when he tries to escape from enemy motor-cyclists who have arrived to occupy the town, and he eventually dies in the flat of a young woman whose own husband is at the front and whose small son has befriended the lost soldier. The story grows out of what Robbe-Grillet was later to call *signes générateurs*: in this case objects like a bayonet or a picture of a military disaster called 'The Defeat at Reichenfels' which the narrator (who is a doctor perhaps, possibly the one called in to treat the wounded soldier) dwells upon in descriptions very similar to those in *Snapshots*; hence my remark earlier that these short texts are structurally and thematically related to the novels written about the same time. Whether the whole novel develops out of a narrator's contemplation of the picture of a café scene after a military defeat, or whether the picture provides an objective correlative of the débâcle in which the doctor indirectly takes part, cannot and need not ultimately be determined.

As in Kafka, this does not mean that nothing can be known for certain. The technique of previous Robbe-Grillet novels – that of returning to scenes previously described and modifying them in respect of some detail or other – is here perfected, but this internal ambiguity is continually being corrected by the care that is taken to pick things up where they were left off, so that a kind of narrative stability develops after all. The soldier's purpose in coming to the town is eventually, if belatedly, explained; in spite of what are referred to as 'small inconsistencies', something reasonably solid is established. This is after all not much different from the way we often have to learn things in life or attempt to recover them from memory; we are often unable to reconstruct events to our entire satisfaction. That is no doubt why Robbe-Grillet insists in his preface that 'the reality here in question is strictly physical' and totally without 'allegorical significance'. He asks that 'the reader should therefore see in it only the objects, the gestures, the words and the events that are told, without seeking to give them either more or less meaning than they would have in his own life, or in his own death' (p. 5). Unfortunately this last phrase about death casts some doubt on whether allegory is being as carefully eschewed as Robbe-Grillet claims, but I think we can give him the benefit of that doubt: the soldier's story is his own and does not imply anything wider about the human condition.

Nevertheless this is a very 'anxious' text, haunted as it says itself by 'exaggeration, and strangeness, and death' (p. 93), by the soldier's nightmares, panic, and fear of labyrinths:

He was dreaming that the alert had sounded. He was in a winding trench, the top of which was on a level with his forehead; in his hand he was holding a sort of elongated grenade whose delayed-action mechanism he had just set off. Without wasting a second he had to throw the thing out of the trench. He could hear the noise of the timing mechanism, like the ticking of a cheap alarm clock. But he just stood there, grenade in hand, his arm stretched out as at the beginning of a throw, but for some inexplicable reason paralysed, becoming more and more rigid, less and less capable of moving even a finger as the moment of the explosion approached. He must have yelled aloud to jerk himself out of the nightmare. (p. 101)

This anxiety reaches its paroxysm as the soldier dies, and the text then gradually calms down, returning in the closing pages to the same elements as in the opening pages:

But the eye mists up as it tries to chart the course of the line, as with the too-fine pattern of the wallpaper and the uncertain outlines of the gleaming paths traced in the dust by the felt slippers, and, beyond the door of the room, the dark hall where the umbrella is leaning at an angle against the coat-stand, then, once past the front door, the succession of long corridors, the spiral staircase, the door of the building with its stone step, and the whole town behind me. (pp. 188–9)

I refer deliberately to the autonomy of the *text* (as opposed to that of the narrator), since Robbe-Grillet is experimenting in this novel with a self-generating work growing out of 'triggers' of various kinds, and even refusing on occasion textual excursions and plot developments that are not considered appropriate. So it makes sense to speak of a form of vertigo in the text itself, a sort of controlled hysteria, which gives Robbe-Grillet's writing its particular flavour and draws us into a world in which anxiety and enigma are not simply thematic concepts but, as in Kafka, organizing and structural elements in their own right. Thus Robbe-Grillet does not merely imitate the externals of Kafka's world – the aspects we think of as particularly 'Kafkaesque', such as claustrophobic mazes and contradictory utterances – he gets right inside it and re-creates it in his own terms. They are those of an atheist who explores guilt without necessarily feeling it himself; but he is happy to owe much to the father-fixated and God-tormented genius who first led the way into the labyrinthine rat-runs of the unquiet mind.

3

LOVE AND LOSS

It is my love that keeps mine eye awake
Mine own true love that doth my rest defeat
To play the watchman ever for thy sake.

(Shakespeare, Sonnet 61)

Robbe-Grillet's most famous novel, *Jealousy* (*La Jalousie*, 1957), turns on a French pun: *la jalousie* is not only jealousy, but the ordinary word for slatted shutters or Venetian blinds. The title itself therefore provides a key to the double meaning which lies at the heart of the book. As Robbe-Grillet himself has explained:

> *La jalousie* is a kind of shutter which allows you to look out and, at certain angles, to look in from outside; but when the slats are closed nothing can be seen in either direction. *La jalousie* is a passion which allows nothing ever to be wiped out: everything seen, however innocent, leaves an indelible trace behind.[16]

Slatted shutters like those Robbe-Grillet describes in *Jealousy* and shows in *The Immortal One* are of course found mostly in hot countries where the light is fierce and maximum ventilation is needed, so it is not surprising that *Jealousy* is set in a tropical banana plantation, and *The Immortal One* in Istanbul. Both texts make much of an observer (the hero) looking in or out of shuttered blinds; in *Jealousy* the husband spies on his wife from the wide balcony of their house as she sits behind the slats in her bedroom, and in *The Immortal One* the lover looks out anxiously on to the street in front of his house to see if the woman he loves is coming to visit him. Both images are highly expressive of the nervous disquiet each man feels about the woman whom he loves and is afraid of losing to another man: the classic situation of jealousy, in fact. In both texts the emotion is created rather than analysed, and objects become the mirrors that reflect back at the hero his fear and anxiety as he enters a vicious circle of ever-increasing tension. So much so that in *Jealousy* the husband cannot be considered normal: he spies on his wife but he is also afraid of her, avoiding her eyes. The only time he can gaze at her freely is when he sees her from behind and she cannot see him. Venetian blinds give him, and the lover in *The Immortal One*, an uneasy sense of security and yet also a voyeuristic feeling of guilt. In this, of course, *Jealousy* takes up where *The Voyeur* left off: the narrator and the voyeur are now one.

Those who are closely scrutinized in *Jealousy* for signs that they are starting an affair are A, the voyeur's wife, and Franck, the owner of a neighbouring plantation. Since the husband tells the story in the third person, he cannot refer to himself as 'I' but instead uses impersonal forms, like 'the moment has come to enquire after Christiane's health' (p. 30), to indicate his own role in the conversation. Similarly the present tense is used extensively throughout, since the husband is living in the continuous present of a strong emotion. The geometric precision and the apparent objectivity – for they are only superficially rational qualities – of the husband's lengthy descriptions of the banana plantation are an attempt to conceal his unease about his relations with his attractive wife. The jealousy is never described, even less analysed: it is shown in the obsessive looking, in the morbid scrutiny of the presumed lovers' least gesture or utterance. It is brilliantly symbolized by the adjustable blinds through which the husband gazes at the woman whose eyes he cannot sustain when she happens to glance in the direction of the position on the other side of the shutters from which he is so closely watching her.

Although Robbe-Grillet claims that no chronological sequence of events can be established by any reading of *Jealousy*, the bare bones of a plot do, in fact, stick out in the skinny body of the novel. All fictions have a shape, even if they go to great

41

lengths, as *Jealousy* does, to conceal it. The narrator disguises the fact that he is telling a story by indulging (the word is chosen deliberately) in detailed, precise descriptions of everything surrounding him, the house and the objects within it, the plantation with its particular arrangement of banana trees, and so on. But he is really interested in what, if anything, is going on between his wife and his neighbour. It is evident, as one would expect, that the two planters and their wives see a lot of each other, but Christiane, Franck's wife, is for some reason not well and no longer accompanies him on visits to the house. This convenient illness arouses the husband's suspicions, and from then on everything that passes between A and Franck is grist to his mill.

To a detached observer there seems at first little to be concerned about, but of course the husband is not a detached observer, and nor can the reader be, since everything is conveyed through the husband's eyes, and his insinuations affect the reader's attitude directly. Over drinks and at dinner the conversation turns on a book, set in Africa, which A is reading and which Franck has lent her. Since the husband does not know the novel they are discussing, he is excluded from their conversation. He watches all the more closely, therefore, for any signs that might betray a growing intimacy between the two, and he thinks he observes the passing of a note. Indeed, rather unusually, the wife seems not to have made herself understood by the native servant, and the husband has to go to fetch ice for their drinks. He suspects that Franck and A have taken advantage of his brief absence from the veranda to plot their next move. This appears to be confirmed when Franck announces that he is driving down to the port to arrange for the purchase of a new lorry, and A immediately suggests that she accompany him to do some shopping. They agree to start around dawn, so as to be able to return the same night; they duly leave together early one morning, but they do not return until the following day.

All the time he is left alone the husband prowls around the house; he searches his wife's room for incriminating evidence, and when in the evening A and Franck fail to return he gives in to his jealous fantasies, even imagining the car in which they are travelling hitting a tree and bursting into flames. When the presumed lovers return the next day, they claim that they had to spend the night in a hotel because Franck's car had, again perhaps conveniently, broken down. A appears, however, no different from her normal immaculate self, but Franck seems embarrassed and makes an ambiguous apology about being an indifferent mechanic (which the husband, of course, takes to refer to his inexpertness as a lover), and he soon takes his leave. Reassured that A is obviously not going to leave him, the husband relaxes and his fit of jealousy subsides. Since the jealous fit is the novel, and the novel a jealous fit, the one ends when the other ends: that is, they subside together into a relatively calm silence. As in neurosis, there are some flickers of the old trouble, but they die away, and the novel closes with a neutral statement: 'Now the dark night and the deafening racket of the crickets once more engulf the garden and the veranda, all around the house' (p. 103).

Although this is a simple outline of the 'story', Robbe-Grillet is right in saying that a precise chronology of the events making it up is impossible to establish, if only because narration and fantasy are inextricably linked, as are different kinds of memory. Indeed, the (relatively trivial) contradictions in the narrative reflect the husband's own uncertainties: he will never know for sure whether in deciding to make the trip to the coast his wife was innocent of adulterous intent or not. Wherever she is, whatever she does, she appears totally at ease, and if she did go to bed with Franck on the night they failed to return nothing in her manner betrays the fact. A page or so before the end the narrator thinks about the novel that Franck and A have discussed so often, but he has only half understood the story and gets into a muddled frenzy over it; likewise he is himself part of, and deeply engaged in, a fiction whose givens are as arbitrary as those of the book Franck and A have been reading. He keeps returning to events he considers significant, such as the letter that A appears to write and pass to Franck; in his mental rehearsal of these occurrences he recalls – or thinks he recalls – different details, but he (or the text which expresses him) is liable to confuse different events, blur temporal distinctions, and even distort reality altogether. He is understandably obsessed with what he has not been able to observe, such as whether A kisses Franck goodbye as she leans inside his car. There are, too, frequent shifts of time in the form of unsignalled flashbacks which mirror the husband's preoccupations, as do the incompatible accounts of the same event which recur in his narrative.

Like all jealous men, he has a highly developed erotic imagination. The well-known description of Franck destroying a centipede in the dining-room watched intently by A, who is herself scrutinized for her reactions by the narrator, is paralleled later in the passage in which the jealous husband imagines Franck killing another insect in the hotel bedroom he shares with A. The analogy is assisted by another double meaning in French; the word *serviette* can mean both table napkin and hand towel. In the first passage, which recounts what actually happened in the dining-room, Franck wads his napkin into a ball and crushes the insect with it, leaving a stain on the wall which later becomes inextricably associated in the narrator's mind with the possibility of a sexual relationship between his wife and his neighbour.

In the second passage, the imaginary one, Franck wads his *serviette* – now a towel – into a ball and squashes the centipede against the bedroom wall. The smooth shift from *serviette* (table napkin) to *serviette de toilette* (hand towel) momentarily disguises from the reader that the narrative has slipped into the imaginary – indeed, into erotic fantasy – in which the wife, excited by Franck's decisive action against the insect, now closes her tapering fingers in a tight grip on the sheet of the bed, whereas before she had been seen (or imagined) to clench the handle of her table knife. Perhaps she was only touching the handle in an automatic gesture, a perfectly natural reaction in the circumstances. Later, however, this gripping action is greatly developed in fantasy:

44

The hand with the tapering fingers has clenched into a fist on the white sheet. The five widespread fingers have closed over the palm with such force that they have drawn the cloth with them: the latter shows five divergent creases . . . (p. 80)

Immediately after this, revealingly, the husband imagines the mosquito-netting falling back all around the lovers' bed, 'interposing the opaque veil of its innumerable meshes where rectangular patches reinforce the torn places', as if to exclude the indiscreet gaze of the guilty observer. Here, as indeed elsewhere, the narrator betrays an awareness that his obsessive scrutiny of his wife is unhealthy, is as much that of a voyeur who wants to spy on sexual activity as of a man who has genuine cause to doubt the fidelity of his companion. To calm himself, he has recourse to describing banana trees.

All of this, of course, makes *Jealousy* a remarkable psychological novel; and yet Robbe-Grillet claims that he has driven psychology out of narrative fiction and left behind a void of non-explanation. But as we can see – and as he himself is well aware – novels about people cannot exclude psychology in the sense of an investigation into or portrayal of human emotions; and, of the emotions traditionally the subject of fiction, jealousy is perhaps the most important. Stendhal in the nineteenth century and Proust in the early decades of this century considerably extended the range and scope of the novel in the handling of love and of jealousy, its concomitant emotion. What Robbe-Grillet has attempted to do – and to my mind has largely succeeded in doing – is to take the novel a step further in the treatment of jealousy from where Proust left it in his masterly but still traditionally discursive analyses of Swann's jealous misery over Odette in *Swann's Way*, and of Marcel's tortured uncertainties about Albertine in *The Captive* and *The Fugitive*. Swann's affair with a woman who made him intensely unhappy, in spite of the fact that she did not really appeal to him and was not even his type – something he can only appreciate when he is no longer jealous over her, which is when

45

he no longer loves her – is described with omniscient detachment in *Swann's Way*. In the later volumes of *A la recherche du temps perdu*, however, it is the narrator himself who is in love and suffers jealousy, this time over Albertine, whom he makes captive in his house.

Robbe-Grillet takes this first-person approach one stage further, by making the jealous husband an observer who recounts the whole business in the third person as if it did not closely concern himself. But of course it does: from this inherent contradiction between the man's emotional involvement and his pseudo-objective stance Robbe-Grillet derives fine effects of irony – ones of which Proust would approve. The contradiction also accounts for the tone of suppressed hysteria, of violent feelings only just contained by a superficially dispassionate manner, which for so many readers is the hallmark of *Jealousy* and helps to explain the book's success around the world. Outside France it is probably the main novel Robbe-Grillet is known by, indeed the only *nouveau roman* that most ordinary readers will have heard of. If my account of it makes it sound quite straightforward, this is because like all profoundly original works of art – *The Waste Land, Ulysses* and *Waiting for Godot* have experienced a similar destiny – the initial iconoclastic impact distracted readers from the basic simplicity of the work's design. This simplicity does not preclude artfulness: the naïve reading Franck and A offer of the 'African' novel is intended as a witty authorial comment on how *not* to read.

Like *The Immortal One*, and like *Marienbad*, *Jealousy* is a love story: the husband notes that the symmetry of his wife's body is perfect, and he cannot take his eyes off the lustrous black curls of her hair as they 'shift with a supple movement and brush her shoulders as she turns her head' (p. 9). Even when tormented by jealousy, he cannot resist citing her witty rejoinders to Franck's frequently crass remarks; for instance, when Franck says that all engines are basically alike, she retorts, 'That's right, like women' (p. 95). Whether or not she is thereby directly implying that Franck is as unsuccessful with motors as he is with women, the narrator clearly savours her answer and Franck's resulting discomfiture, just as he enjoys the spectacle of Franck's embarrassment when A suggests, apropos of the novel they are reading, that there is nothing wrong with a white woman sleeping with blacks. This amorously respectful treatment of A by the narrator – like his erotic awareness of sounds that resemble a lover's cries, and of A's abandoned poses when she lies down on her bed – show how intensely involved with her he is. *Jealousy* is a disturbing journey to the dark side of the moon of love: the story of a love which is doubtful, tormented and unhappy, but which suffers and perhaps survives nevertheless.

The Immortal One (*L'Immortelle*, 1963), on the other hand, is an account of a love affair which ends in loss. This profoundly characteristic work was Robbe-Grillet's first film to be both scripted and directed by himself; it has inevitably been overshadowed by *Marienbad* (which was conceived later but released earlier, since shooting of *The Immortal One* on location in Turkey had to be postponed for political reasons) because of Alain Resnais's highly praised direction of the *Marienbad* script. There is inevitably a certain amateurish clumsiness on the part of the author-director (in particular, the actors were required to behave with a degree of formality and lack of expressiveness which to the spectator seems not only unnatural but positively wooden), but this is compensated in large part by a mythical substructure that makes the film a moving experience. It is a retelling of the legend of Orpheus and Eurydice, and once again the basic plot is clear enough.

N, a teacher recently arrived in Istanbul from France, meets a mysterious and beautiful young woman referred to in the text as L. She speaks perfect French but she claims not to be French; in fact, her nationality is never revealed. When they meet she seems to be in the company of a thick-set older man, referred to as M (perhaps her *mari*, husband, or *maquereau*, pimp), who is always accompanied by a pair of large and vicious guard dogs. N and L have a tender but brief love affair, towards the end of which L seems tense and anxious, especially when the barking of dogs is heard. One day while she is visiting some old fortifications with N, a small boy comes to deliver a message to her in Greek, which of course N cannot understand. The boy tells her that 'he' is back and has asked where she is. L replies in Greek that she will be back in ten minutes, and immediately takes her leave of N. She fails to turn up at their rendezvous a few days later, and he embarks on a search for her, asking several people who seem to know her to help him find her, but they either are unwilling to get involved or try to warn him off. Then one night he suddenly meets her in the street, where she seems to be soliciting in the company of M. When he seeks an explanation for her disappearance, she leads him to her car and drives off with him into the night. They pass his house, but she sees a man who seems to be one of M's spies, and so drives on, faster and faster. Round a bend she comes face to face with one of M's dogs, and she swerves to avoid it. The car crashes into a tree and lands up in the ditch. N is only slightly injured, but the dog is dead – and so, tragically, is L.

The police take no interest in the case, treating it as a straightforward car accident, and other people prove equally uncooperative as N once again sets about trying to find out more about L. N relives in imagination their brief affair, especially its more erotic aspects, and finally buys a white Buick very similar to the one she was driving when she was killed. It is as if he were trying to rejoin her by re-enacting her final moments; he too drives off into the night, passes M on the road holding one of his dogs on a lead, and then confronts the other dog standing in the middle of the road, and is killed in the same way as L was. The film ends with a shot of L seen full-length, looking straight at the camera – which tends to be the eye of N himself – on the deck of a ferry on the Bosphorus. She is wearing a black, rather formal dress, as if in mourning for them both, and bursts into a gay but silent laugh, which soon vanishes from her face as her features resume their familiar seriousness of expression to the accompaniment of a sad and tender Turkish song heard on the sound-track. This Orpheus, having lost his Eurydice to Hades, and failing to resurrect her other than in his fantasies, joins her in death via a car crash which is identical to her own.

She is immortal, indeed, because she lives on in his eroticized consciousness, and he has in a sense already died with her in the first crash: while he is investigating her death he is told, by a woman who bears a close physical resemblance to her, that L's companion – that is, he himself – was killed with her after seizing the wheel and throwing the car against a tree. 'Why would he do that?' N asks. 'I don't know. . . . Out of jealousy,' the woman replies (p. 158). Although she is wrong about the circumstances, her prediction turns out to be correct in its essentials. And, just as his death is prophesied, L's life with him is relived with heightened intensity as he goes in search of her. He pins a simple drawing of a tulip above his bed after she has gone because she had said that her name meant tulip, and this piece of paper comes to symbolize his lost love, as do the Turkish flutes heard spasmodically on the sound-track. The sound of dogs barking puts an abrupt end to the plaintive music of the flutes, and this clearly indicates the threat which hovers over their love affair. In fact, sound and image interact closely throughout the film to suggest a story that the actual shots tend to contradict, but only because memory, and fantasy embroidering on past events, tend to distort reality; once the spectator has adjusted to the grammar of narrative at work, there is little difficulty in following a film which appeals directly to the emotions and is puzzling only to the intellect.

In this appeal to the emotions, there is first of all the setting, 'un décor d'opérette pour une histoire d'amour' (p. 75), the exotic, romantic and mysterious world of old Byzantium and the 'legendary land of Turkey' with its 'mosques, castles, secret gardens and harems' (p. 25), the magical east of one's dreams. Then there are the popular songs of Istanbul played on the sound-track, 'sung by a woman with a deep, sensuous voice, a beautiful voice with heart-rending inflections, very typical of modern Turkish popular music [and] known as *alla turca*' (p. 11). Finally there is the coolly beautiful actress who plays L, Françoise Brion, whose face can express anxious seriousness at

49

one moment and deep relaxation the next; her smile, as she yields to N's advances, is 'tender, docile and enigmatic' (p. 45), and though she later lets him take her hand as they walk through the popular quarters of Istanbul she is unwilling to be kissed in public, and indeed the sight of a dropped curtain in a nearby window warns both of them that this would be unwise. After he has taken her to a night-club where they watch a dancer execute an erotic 'oriental' number, she later performs an imitation of the dance for his benefit in the intimacy of his room, just as on another occasion she undresses seductively for him, and after they have made love gazes tenderly into his eyes.

If this sympathetic, even somewhat romantic treatment of love seems incongruous in Robbe-Grillet – at least as he is usually portrayed by critics and indeed by himself – the simple truth is that this is what the published scenario (the *ciné-roman*) reveals. The film version is inevitably more ambiguous, but even there the impression is powerfully conveyed of a man in a strange country falling in love with a woman who may be some kind of prostitute and who burns her fingers when she too falls in love, perhaps because he represents a different kind of life for her. The chain she wears occasionally twined around her neck perhaps symbolizes her enslavement, as the colours of the flowers the Lady of the Camellias wore indicated to her lovers the time of the month and thus whether she was available or not. If L is such a courtesan, N either fails to read the warning signals or chooses to ignore them. But, as other people tell him, he would do well to be careful, since he does not know the ways of this country and particularly how dangerous it is to provoke jealous husbands or protectors. But N is very much the innocent abroad who does not understand the local language and customs. He is also a kind of Everyman, grappling with the enigmas of his situation, and if his difficulties are never resolved, if he finds himself a helpless spectator of tragic events, it is because he is only an ordinary individual and lacks the necessary strength to overcome the obstacles and the men who block his path and foil his quest with quite deliberate guile.

The Immortal One is perhaps Robbe-Grillet's least-known

work; the film soon passed into oblivion and the book has sold fewer copies in France than any of his other works. Nevertheless it is, as I have said, a profoundly characteristic creation which breaks down the distinction between subjectivity and objectivity by telling a story that combines a firm narrative line on the one hand and, on the other, the necessary confusions, ambiguities and uncertainties within an individual consciousness, that of the observer and narrator N. Because the situation is seen through the eyes of a participant who by definition cannot understand precisely what is going on, the spectator cannot expect to have everything revealed either. But this does not prevent the audience experiencing a deeply moving story of love and loss.

The same is true of *Last Year at Marienbad* (*L'Année dernière à Marienbad*, 1961), which was as big a commercial success as *The Immortal One* was a flop. It deserved a triumph because it is a much better film, directed by one of the great artists of the French *nouvelle vague*, Alain Resnais, who gave a superbly sensitive and authoritative rendering of Robbe-Grillet's script. It is, as Robbe-Grillet himself has said, the story of a persuasion. A stranger – designated simply as X – wanders through an exclusive international hotel where the camera keeps returning to the face of a young woman, to whom X offers a very seductive gift, 'a past, a future, and freedom' (p. 9). He tells her that she and he had met and fallen in love the previous year at Marienbad. Now he has come, he tells her, to the rendezvous she herself had arranged a year ago, and in accordance with their agreement he is going to take her away with him. That is precisely what then happens. At first the woman (referred to as A) treats the matter as a joke; then she wonders if he is not suffering from delusions; but finally she yields to his persuasion, accepts his version of what took place 'last year at Marienbad', and leaves the hotel in his company. As Robbe-Grillet comments:

> She already has yielded, in fact, long since. After a final attempt to resist, to offer her protector [the French word is

gardien – literally, 'keeper' – and he is designated once again as M] a last chance of winning her back, she seems to accept the identity the stranger offers her, and agrees to go with him towards something, something unnamed, something *other*: love, poetry, freedom . . . or perhaps death . . . (p. 10)

This is because the past that X appeals to 'has no reality beyond the moment it is evoked with sufficient force; and, when it finally triumphs, it has quite simply become the present, as if it had never ceased to be so' (p. 11).

Like the other works discussed in this chapter, *Marienbad* is a triangle: there are three main characters, a woman, a lover or potential lover, and a husband or protector. It differs from them in stressing that love is a labyrinth, a maze of 'false trails, variants, failures and repetitions' (p. 9), paralleled in the labyrinthine series of corridors and salons in the hotel and in the interiors in which no window is to be seen, only mirrors. The landscape outside is never seen from within, and this symbolizes the claustrophobic nature of A's situation, hemmed in as she is by X's insistence and M's over-protective concern. The formal gardens surrounding the hotel do not offer a real exterior either, but X implies, as he and A leave the hotel together, that they will vanish into it for ever:

> The park of this hotel was a kind of garden *à la française* without any trees or flowers, without any foliage. . . . Gravel, stone, marble, straight lines, marked out rigid spaces, surfaces without mystery. It seemed, at first glance, impossible to get lost there . . . at first glance . . . down straight paths, between the statues with frozen gestures and the granite slabs, where you were now already getting lost, for ever, in the calm night, alone with me. (p. 151)

M, who has beaten X several times at the Chinese game of Nim, in which the player who picks up the last card loses, is paradoxically – and ironically – outmanœuvred by X in the struggle to capture or keep A; in that deadly serious game, the contestant who takes the last 'card' is in fact the winner. As X suggests, M is defeated not so much by X's skill as a seducer as by his own world-weariness. X believes passionately in the truth of his story about what took place last year at Marienbad, and his conviction proves infectious to A; M, on the other hand, does not seem to feel passionately about anything. This is an interesting reversal of the situation in *Jealousy*, where it is as much the husband's powerful and adoring insistence as Franck's apparent inexpertness as a lover which keeps A faithful to him.

In 1961, during the final stages of the making of *Marienbad*, Robbe-Grillet wrote a script for a large Japanese production company who mistakenly thought he was a popular writer. They were so taken aback by the shooting script that Robbe-Grillet submitted that they asked him to make extensive changes which would have brought the story more into line with commercial norms. He refused, and the film was never made. Nevertheless a synopsis and a couple of extracts were published in the Robbe-Grillet special issue of the review *Obliques* in 1978. Once again three people are involved: Aya, a young Japanese woman studying medicine in a French-speaking country in Europe, Jean, a fellow student, and Claire, Jean's girlfriend. Jean starts giving Aya French conversation lessons and falls in love with her, but Claire is jealous and sows the seeds of discord between them. Jean is finally driven to murder Aya 'in a paroxysm of doubt and desire. . . . Jean thought he was teaching Aya to love, whereas the Japanese girl thought she was only learning French; in fact, she was learning to die' (*Ob.*, p. 44).

Not only does this synopsis reveal Robbe-Grillet's perhaps surprising interest in the issue of an appropriate pedagogy for French – something that also surfaces in *Djinn* (1981) – but it also takes up again the question of destructive jealousy and of the close association between love and death, especially violent death, which was the theme of *The Immortal One*. It is also like *The Immortal One* in being circular: N, before he died, met the woman who looked like L in circumstances identical to those of his original encounter with L, and in *La Japonaise* – the title of the film that was never made – Aya lies after her death in a posture very similar to that in which her best friend was left on being trampled to death by a Tokyo crowd which had gone berserk. *Marienbad* is circular too, in that the play being performed in the little theatre of the hotel at the beginning of the film recurs at the end, when the parallel between the situation enacted on stage between the actors and the imminent flight of A with X is, like the play-within-the-play in *Hamlet*, the occasion of a fine touch of dramatic irony.

A last unmade film, also summarized in *Obliques*, shares similar characteristics. *Le Magicien* dates from 1964 and is another three-cornered drama involving a film director, his young actress wife and a handsome 30-year-old actor. Since there is a parallel film-within-the-film, the situation is not dissimilar to the Pinter/Reisz version of John Fowles's *The French Lieutenant's Woman*, and Robbe-Grillet is clearly fascinated, as is Harold Pinter, with different levels of narrative discourse and with the interaction between realities which continually refer to each other. The basic 'architecture of the drama' Robbe-Grillet has summarized as follows:

A husband who is deeply in love with his young but too compliant wife thrusts her into the arms of another man; he organizes their relationship, he fixes each word, every intonation, each gesture and every look with the precision of a madman. . . . He wishes her to seduce the other man and wants the latter, torn between desire and revulsion, to reject her advances. But at the last moment, carried away by love perhaps for the other whom she has come too close to, she engineers an accident in which her husband is killed. (*Ob.*, p. 261)

The film-within-the-film ends with the death of a dancer (played by the wife) followed by the suicide of a composer (played by the handsome lead), and the 'outer' film closes on a shot of the actor and actress, after the death of the director, watching the finished print. 'As the body of the murdered dancer appears on the screen, the actor gives his companion an odd look and takes her hand in his own' (*Ob.*, p. 261), incidentally prefiguring the end of *Trans-Europ-Express*.

With its theme of death and resurrection, *Le Magicien* is the exact opposite of *The Immortal One*, at least at the level of plot; but, as we saw, *The Immortal One* is at another level also about art and immortality: L cannot die because she lives on in the print of the film as she has been resurrected in her lover's erotic imagination. And further back, of course, the design of *Le Magicien* recalls that of one of the great novels of modernism, Gide's *The Counterfeiters* (1925), the story of a novelist who is writing a novel called *The Counterfeiters*. Not all the works I have discussed in this chapter attain that degree of complexity; but what they do all clearly have in common is the same plangent threnody of love and loss.

4

SEX AND STEREOTYPE

Eroticism is the supreme game: it's tough, it's severe and it's
deadly serious. (Interview comment)

Apart from Delvaux, no other artist so haunts Robbe-Grillet's
world as does Gustave Moreau (1826–98), the great symbolist
painter whose vision of vampire-women like Salome preying
on male victims in a morbid atmosphere of lust and luxury,
masochism and death opened the way not only for the erotic
antinomies of Munch and Strindberg but also for the surreal
inventions of Breton and Magritte, whence the line continues
directly to Robbe-Grillet himself. It is therefore not surprising
that 'The Secret Room' ('La Chambre secrète'), a short text of
1962 collected in *Snapshots*, not only should be dedicated to
Moreau but is directly inspired by his paintings and his
'ébauches de débauches' (as Pierre Schneider has wittily called
his water-colour sketches).[17]

The text recounts a sort of ritual murder in a setting typical
of Moreau's brightly coloured indoor world:

> In the background, towards the top of the staircase, a black
> silhouette is moving further away, a man enveloped in a
> long, flowing cloak, who is climbing the last steps without
> looking back, his task fulfilled. A tenuous column of smoke
> rises in spirals from a sort of incense-burner placed on a high,
> wrought-iron stand with silvery highlights. The milky body
> is lying quite near, with the broad trickles of blood running
> from the left breast down the side and on the hip.
>
> It is the body of a woman, full-figured but not heavy, quite
> naked, lying on her back, her bust slightly raised by thick
> cushions thrown on to the ground, which is covered with

rugs of oriental design. Her waist is very narrow, her neck long and slim, bent over to one side, her head thrown back into a darker area in which the features can nevertheless be divined; the half-open mouth, the big, open eyes, fixed and shining, and the mass of long, black hair, spread out in waves of well-regulated disorder on a material, perhaps velvet, with heavy folds, on which the arm and shoulder are also lying. (*STNN*, pp. 35–6)

The text moves forward and backward in time, so that later the woman's body is described as it was before the sacrifice: 'the black tuft of hair and the white stomach, the soft curve of the hips, the narrow waist and, higher up, the nacreous breasts which rise and fall to the rhythm of the rapid breathing' (*STNN*, p. 39), and then the murder is described in detail.

'The Secret Room' is typical of most of Robbe-Grillet's novels and films since the mid-sixties, but obsession with the sadistic killing of women goes back to *The Voyeur* at least; indeed, there is a very short text, dating from several years before work started on *The Voyeur*, which describes the ritual murder of a little girl. Performed with a stiletto, this resembles the sexual act with intense excitement on both sides, and the little girl goes to heaven where she will become her killer's 'guardian angel', soothing away all the weariness and grief in the man's life (*Ob.*, p. 93).

There is also the pornographic novel which Robbe-Grillet probably had a hand in writing, *L'Image*, by an anonymous author or authors whose sobriquet is 'Jean de Berg', a name that crops up in *Topology of a Phantom City*; since Robbe-Grillet makes something of a trademark of using the same fictional names on different occasions, he is slyly admitting that he wrote *L'Image*, or at least had a lot to do with it. Paris literary gossip would have one believe that Catherine Robbe-Grillet is the author, but the most likely explanation of the different styles that make up the novel is that a group of friends put the book together, led or at least encouraged by Robbe-

De Berg

Grillet himself. One section bears all the marks of Robbe-Grillet's manner, and his wife and others may well have done the rest.[18] The book (published in 1956) is dedicated to Pauline Réage, the pseudonymous author of *Story of O* (*Histoire d'O*, 1954), and the rather joky preface, signed 'P.R.', may possibly have been written by her. Unfortunately the reference to *Story of O* serves merely to demonstrate by contrast what a masterpiece of sustained mysticism – and even, paradoxically, of incandescent purity – Réage's book is. Apart from being second-rate pornography, *L'Image* projects a view of sexuality that has come to be referred to as 'sexploitation'. The author(s) create an unreal pornotopia, such as the one Steven Marcus has described in *The Other Victorians* (1966), his study of sexuality and pornography in Victorian England.

Robbe-Grillet's view of women's sexuality seems at best misleading and at worse sadistic and perverse, and his attempts in articles and interviews to argue that he is being ironic, self-aware and amusedly detached from these phantasms are not wholly convincing. Another pornographic work of his, signed this time with his own name and that of the photographer Irina Ionesco, *Temple aux miroirs* (1977), is sold in a sealed polythene cover and shows an obsessive and repellent interest in the genitals of little girls. Paedophilia, voyeurism and sadism are indeed the hallmarks of most of the works considered in this chapter, which are therefore not for the squeamish.

Robbe-Grillet claims that he is fascinated by images and stereotypes, especially those of a popular nature, and this is borne out by his pastiche of the detective story in *The Erasers*, for example, or of the resistance war film in *L'Homme qui ment*. He has written a preface for a photo-novel by Edward Lachman and Elieba Levine called *Chausse-trappes* (1981), and the book represents what he calls the second degree of that popular French form the *roman-photo* (a sort of cross between the comic strip and the feature film), just as *Souvenirs du triangle d'or* is the second degree of a Mickey Spillane or James

Hadley Chase hard-boiled sex-and-crime thriller; in *Souvenirs*, as George Orwell said of Chase's 'cruel and corrupt' books, 'there are no gentlemen and no taboos'.[19]

But the danger with this indulgence in stereotypes, as Roy Armes has pointed out, is that Robbe-Grillet's 'parodistic non-narratives come perilously close to the very objects they are parodying and are indeed marketed as the real thing; [they] constitute a questionable advance for an artist whose abiding interest has always been with formal structures.'[20] Revealingly, Robbe-Grillet has implicitly compared himself with men in Turkey who stare at western women and 'follow, with motionless intensity, the outline of their bodies under their summer dresses, down to their unfettered ankles, and pursue an inward dream which would make them captive, chained up within a magic circle' (*Ob.*, p. 228). Such a notion, on the part of a citizen of a civilized country which protects women as far as possible from male violence, might seem merely harmless frivolity; but I think that, were I a woman, I would consider it not only nonsense, but dangerous and pernicious nonsense. This is, however, something every reader will decide for him or herself, and in what follows the discussion will be as neutral, morally speaking, as possible. In reading him we may like to give Robbe-Grillet the benefit of the doubt that his kind of sado-eroticism is purely imaginary and that, far from being able to be satisfied by explicit activity, it can only exist at the level of fantasy.

The work that drew out Robbe-Grillet's preoccupation with sadistic pornography in the way 'The Secret Room' had indicated was *The House of Assignation* (*La Maison de rendez-vous*, 1965). This has been followed by a number of similar novels and films of which the most recent at the time of writing is *La Belle Captive*, a film released in 1983. I shall take them in turn, although, in order to avoid repetition as far as possible, some of them will be only briefly discussed. Although Robbe-Grillet's technique is always dazzlingly inventive, the content tends to duplicate itself.

For the first work in this sequence, Robbe-Grillet chose an

appropriately exotic setting, Hong Kong. It will be remembered that he provided a preface to *In the Labyrinth* which warned the reader against an allegorical interpretation; he provides not one but two prefatory notes to *The House of Assignation*, and they deliberately cancel each other out:

> The author wishes to make it clear that this novel is in no way intended to be an account of life in the British territory of Hong Kong. Any resemblance, in setting or situation, between the two is a matter of pure coincidence, whether objective or otherwise. (p. 5)

That is the first, and it contains a wink at the reader who is familiar with the surrealist notion of *hasard objectif*. The second reads as follows:

> Should any reader, knowing his Far-Eastern ports well, form the opinion that the places described here do not correspond to reality, the author, who has himself spent the greater part of his life there, would advise him to go back and look again: things change quickly in those parts. (p. 7)

The paradox is to some extent resolved by Robbe-Grillet's belief that the life of the imagination is the true life of man. The Hong Kong most people carry around in their minds is, and is not, a real place in the South China Sea. Robbe-Grillet sets out to develop the fantasy image most people have of the colony: of a place where the clandestine traffic in opium and girls overshadows the better-known legitimate forms of trade, and where money will buy anything, and particularly any sexual indulgence, however outlandish.[21]

The stereotypes in this novel are the Villa Bleue, the high-class brothel which is the house of assignation in the title, a character called Sir Ralph who could come straight out of the pages of *Story of O*, and suggestions of perverse sexual practices such as cannibalism, particularly the consumption of the flesh of young girls. The story is a contradictory one – basically, Johnson has to leave Hong Kong in a hurry after the murder of his associate Manneret, wishes to take Lauren, one of the Villa Bleue prostitutes, with him, asks Manneret for the huge sum demanded for this favour, kills his associate when this is refused, and so has to leave Hong Kong in a hurry – indeed, it is the kind of closed circle which Robbe-Grillet was perhaps thinking of in *The Voyeur* when Mathias sees a film poster advertising a showing of 'Mr X on the Double Circuit'. Since Johnson, alias Sir Ralph, makes the mistake of returning to the Villa Bleue to collect Lauren, only to find the British police waiting in ambush for him, the book is almost a simple tale of a successful arrest using the gangster's moll as the decoy:

> It is only when he is in the middle of the room that he sees the police lieutenant in khaki shorts and white socks. He whirls round and sees that the door has shut behind him and that a soldier holding a machine-gun is standing in front of it, barring the way. More slowly now, his eye sweeps the whole room. The second soldier, who is by the closed curtains of the bay-window, is also watching him attentively, holding his machine-gun with both hands, trained on him. The lieutenant does not move either and does not take his eyes off him. Lauren is lying on the fur bedspread, between the four pillars that support the tester over her like a canopy. She is wearing pyjamas of golden silk that hug the lines of her body, with a small stand-up collar and long sleeves, in the Chinese style. She is lying on her side with one knee flexed and the other leg stretched out, her head raised on one elbow, looking at him without a single gesture, without moving a single feature of her smooth face. And there is nothing in her eyes. (pp. 125–6)

I say 'almost' because, much as the book owes to such stereotypes as the James Bond films, it is not in itself a coherent narrative; indeed, inconsistency is built into it as the organizing principle of the text. It would be easy to treat the whole thing as a witty literary exercise, were it not for such inconvenient facts about Hong Kong as the following, which came to light in

61

1982, many years after the publication of *The House of Assignation*, and was reported briefly in *The Times*:

Human organs found in flat

Hongkong (Reuter) – A taxi driver and his brother were charged with murder yesterday after police found preserved female sex organs in their flat.

Local newspapers said parts of at least three women were found, and that cannibalism was a possibility being investigated. Also seized were hundreds of photographs of female bodies being cut up.[22]

Another instance, perhaps, of life imitating art? Perhaps things do indeed change quickly in that part of the world.

The House of Assignation, it should be said, is a 'good read'; in fact it is probably Robbe-Grillet's most attractive and amusing work. Although, like the books it imitates, it deals with a serious subject, crime, it handles it in a manner which is neither serious nor frivolous. Indeed, unlike some of the books it parodies, it has a refreshing knack of not taking itself too seriously. How could it, with an opening like this, which dwells on such Robbe-Grillet erotic clichés as the nape of the neck and dressmaker's dummies?

Women's flesh has in all probability always played a large part in my dreams. Even when awake my mind is constantly assailed by images of it. A girl in a summer dress presents the curved nape of her neck – she is fastening her sandal – her hair thrown half forward to reveal the delicate skin and its pale down. Immediately I see her pressed into granting some favour and my imagination is unleashed. The narrow hobble-skirt, slit up to the thighs, which is worn by the smart women of Hong Kong, is suddenly ripped by a violent hand, baring the firm, rounded, smooth, gleaming hip and the tender hollow of the small of the back. The leather whip in the window of a Paris saddler, the bare breasts of a dressmaker's dummy, a half-clad figure on a poster, an advertisement for suspenders or for a perfume, two moist, parted lips, a metal bracelet or a dog's collar impose on me their insistent, provocative décor. (p. 9)

After *The House of Assignation* Robbe-Grillet made three films, each more radical in technique than the last: *Trans-Europ-Express* (1966), which treats the underworld of Antwerp – with its complex rivalries and settling of scores – rather like that of Hong Kong in *The House of Assignation*; *L'Homme qui ment* (1968), which is set in Czechoslovakia and pastiches the familiar story of a partisans' resistance movement in the last war; and *L'Eden et après* (1970). This, his first colour film, was marked by the overt use of sexual stereotypes, and by the female nude treated with the surreal matter-of-factness of Delvaux, just as *Trans-Europ-Express* lifts whole sequences from pornographic 'bondage' magazines. For none of these films has Robbe-Grillet wished to publish a 'cine-novel', so that there is not much that can be said about them in a literary study like this. Nevertheless it is clear from the synopses and fragments that have been published, as well as from recollections of the screenings of the pictures themselves, that these are at once highly erotic and aesthetically sophisticated films which have, however, failed to please either the pornography addict or the art-cinema enthusiast.

Robbe-Grillet returned to prose fiction with *Project for a Revolution in New York* (*Projet pour une révolution à New York*) in 1970. This time the stereotype is the American gangster story and indeed the whole myth of urban violence in the United States. There is a deliberate irony in talking about 'revolution' in a monotonously regular world such as that of New York in the late 1960s – indeed, in a world in which erotic activity of the most sadistic kind, rather than anything remotely resembling revolutionary politics, is at the centre of the book. Robbe-Grillet's New York is a world of subways, high buildings, narrow streets and endless fire-escapes, urban rather than specifically American, and no more like the real city of New York than his Hong Kong in *The House of Assignation* is like the British colony in southern China. It is easy to be highminded about this and say – as Pierre Bourgeade did in *Le Monde* when the book was published – that to 'cover a shoddy sadism and a racist discourse with a commercial title, which seems to designate all those who are truly preparing the revolution in New York, is an act of blatant provocation.'[23] But what strikes the Anglo-Saxon reader is not so much the inappropriateness of the title as the naïve image of the United States which the book projects, and it seems to such a reader curious that French intellectuals – Sartre too, interestingly enough – manage to visit a country whose language they do not speak, and even live there, without for a moment really understanding it. Of course New York is a violent city; but it is also a beautiful and well-ordered one, and to read Robbe-Grillet you would never guess so. Although not intended as a realistic account, *Project* is a disappointing, even silly book, another example of the way Europeans have been obsessed by, but have failed to understand, the myth of America, preferring instead to turn stock images and tropes into transfigurations of the fantastic.[24]

Robbe-Grillet's next work – one is conscious of a declining spiral – was *Glissements progressifs du plaisir*, a film released at the same time as the cine-novel in 1974. It was restricted to spectators over 18 because according to the French film censor it contained 'explicit scenes of cruelty and perversion', set this time in a girls' prison run by nuns. Here the images derive, as Robbe-Grillet says, 'from the Middle Ages of popular fiction in which, under the impassive gaze of a ruling nun, lesbian love affairs, ritual humiliations and the tortures of the Inquisition flourish' (p. 19). The film creates a world of 'bonds, fire, kisses, knives and bites' (p. 19) which draws so freely on the clichés of pornography as to leave the spectator wondering if there is any difference. Although the story is more complex than 'sexploitation' movies usually are, being (somewhat in the manner of *Le Magicien*) about a transfer of roles leading to a fatal accident, the direction is so pornographically self-indulgent as to alienate all but the most devoted spectators.

Topology of a Phantom City (Topologie d'une cité fantôme,

1976) is really a collection of discrete prose texts, some of which first appeared in the two books of photographs for which Robbe-Grillet provided the text and David Hamilton (who is mentioned by name in *Topology*) the plates. *Dreams of Young Girls* (*Rêves de jeunes filles*) first came out in 1971 and *Sisters* (*Les Demoiselles d'Hamilton*) in 1972, and both contain the soft-focus, rather 'soft-porn' pictures that are characteristic of Hamilton and are widely known through posters and postcards. But *Topology* also contains pieces written for illustrated books by Paul Delvaux and René Magritte, and these are clearly derived from the surrealistic images of both painters. Since the book written with Magritte – *La Belle Captive* (1975) – also contains a fragment from Robbe-Grillet's most recent novel to date, *Souvenirs du triangle d'or* (1978), which itself reprints material from the erotic photograph album *Temple aux miroirs* mentioned earlier, the works of the late 1970s not only interrelate but seem to feed off each other, as if – to quote the blurb of *Souvenirs*, obviously written by Robbe-Grillet himself – they were 'indulging in sado-erotic practices with the body of their own narrative', an incestuousness which once again is not accidental, or the result of shortage of material, but an organizing principle in itself.

The principal stereotype in *Topology* and *Souvenirs* (apart, that is, from the ubiquitous female triangle) is apocalyptic writing of the sort made popular by J. G. Ballard. Indeed, the imagery of crashed or abandoned cars in *Topology* may well have been influenced by Ballard's black piece of pornographic fantasy *Crash* (1973), which has enjoyed some success in French translation, and which warns against dehumanized eroticism and the brutality made possible by technology. In the 'incipit' to *Topology* the narrator describes how he imagines the phantom city, and the terms he uses are distinctly apocalyptic:

Before I fall asleep, still stubbornly persistent, the dead city . . .
 Right. I am alone. It is late. I am keeping watch. The last

watchman after the rain, after the fire, after the war, I listen still through endless thicknesses of white ice for the imperceptible, absent sounds: the last crackings of burnt walls, a thin stream of ash or dust pouring from a split, water dripping in a cellar with a fractured vault, a stone coming loose from the gutted façade of a large and important-looking building, tumbling down, bouncing from projection to cornice to roll on the ground among the other stones. (p. 9)

Robbe-Grillet's 'rituals of violence and representation' (p. 33) constitute a deliberately joky apocalypse. In fact what is striking about Robbe-Grillet — and the same point can be made about aspects of the work of other major contemporary novelists such as John Hawkes or Angela Carter — is that, although he deals with extreme states and even nightmare, he is developing a form of fiction which is increasingly *meta*textual. Robbe-Grillet is very conscious of the fact that a novel has to end, for instance. The writing of the end of a book is different in kind from the writing of the beginning, he says, because the text itself becomes conscious, as it were, that the end is near, that time has run out and that the material is exhausted, that possibilities of prolongation have to be eschewed. The phenomenon is treated in an ironical manner in the closing pages of *Project*, where the word 'cat' crops up but is turned aside as an obtrusive irrelevance at this late stage in the proceedings:

I still had left to describe, in the same order of ideas, the fourth act of the torture of Joan, the pretty milky-skinned whore. But time is short. Soon it will be day. And now there has just appeared a 'cat' somewhere in the sentence, apropos of Sarah the half-caste: a deaf man and a cat. The deaf man, I'm convinced, is the trumpet player at 'Old Joe's'. But the cat has not yet played any part here, to my knowledge; so that can only be a mistake . . . it is too late. (p. 177)

We have come a long way from the Book of Revelation – the

text – to works like *Project for a Revolution in New York* which are its metatext, and from John's triumphant ending 'Even so, come, Lord Jesus' to Robbe-Grillet's peremptory 'faster, please, faster!' (p. 180) as his narrator hastens, in an interesting twist on Frank Kermode's *Sense of an Ending*, to wrap it up, close the fictional shop and go home. Robbe-Grillet has perhaps, in these last three novels, written the ultimate apocalyptic work: fictions about the end that bring themselves to an end in wry commentary upon the entire genre of doom fiction, which derives from John of Patmos and which has known in recent decades such an extraordinary renaissance as a reminder of a catastrophe that may be lying in wait for all of us. This could, however, be putting it too loftily. Whatever else may be said about him, Robbe-Grillet does not take himself too seriously, and the metatextual variations of his latest phase will doubtless strike many readers as owing more to the Marquis de Sade's fantasies than they do to John of Patmos's excoriating vision of the end of all things.

5

THEORY AND PRACTICE

I went upstairs again and sat in my chair thinking about
Harry Jones and his story. It seemed a little too pat. It had the
austere simplicity of fiction rather than the tangled woof of
fact. (Raymond Chandler, *The Big Sleep*)

The last chapter showed that the interest of Robbe-Grillet's
work, in terms of its subject-matter at least, is declining fast as
he indulges more and more exclusively in a kind of sophisticated sado-erotic pornography. But fortunately his earlier
radical novels remain radical, and his theoretical writings of
the 1950s and early 1960s are of abiding interest. They were
collected in *Towards a New Novel* (*Pour un nouveau roman*,
1963), of which Martin Seymour-Smith has said that it gathers
together into one polemic 'nearly all the concerns of fictional
modernism', and Frank Kermode that it is 'one of the really
important contributions to the theory of the novel'.[25] The
essays do not constitute a systematic analysis, since they were
written at different times and for different journals, but they do
add up to a singleminded group of statements which, taken
together, show remarkable unity of tone and purpose.

Although Robbe-Grillet has a lot to say in them about
literature, especially literature as he believed it had to be
written in the wake of *Ulysses*, *The Castle* and *The Sound and
the Fury*, the roots of his polemic lie not so much in aesthetics as
in metaphysics. His most deeply felt and strongly held views
are contained in those passages which deal with humanity's
relationship to the universe. Robbe-Grillet takes as his premiss
a thoroughgoing atheism, a conviction that we are alone in the
universe and that there is no God of any kind to grant us the
continuity we so grievously lack, or rather so grieve to lack. But

the fact that no absolute certainty is available does not imply chaos. Man's activities on earth, Robbe-Grillet believes, will always 'remain on a human scale and will be of importance only to man', and he goes on to insist that 'he will not in this way attain any sort of essence of things', and that 'the creation to which we are being invited will have to be perpetually begun anew, by us, and by those who come after us' (*STNN*, pp. 117–18). In other words, we create only for ourselves and for our descendants, deal only with the here and now so far as we ourselves are concerned, and so in literary activity must be firmly subjective:

> It is only God who can claim to be objective. While in my books, on the contrary, it is a *man* who sees, who feels, who imagines, a man who is situated in time and space, conditioned by his emotions, a man like you and me. (*STNN*, p. 139)

Since for Robbe-Grillet there is no God, objectivity in literature – especially that attempted by the use of an omniscient, omnipresent narrator who is a kind of literary pseudo-God – is an impossibility, and has to be discarded together with the 'old myths of "depth"' on which all fiction, he claims, used to be based. Now, however, 'essentialist conceptions of man face their doom, and the idea of "condition" henceforth replac[es] that of "nature".' The surface of things has stopped being 'the mask of their heart' for us, a sentiment which once served, he says, as a prelude 'to all the "beyonds" of metaphysics' (*STNN*, pp. 56–7). For readers were reassured by the notion that nature had depths which human beings alone could plumb: far from this 'sacred vertigo' which overwhelmed them causing any distress or nausea, they were on the contrary reassured by their powers of domination over the world and by their ability to gain access to the hidden soul of things.

Because it was not at first clearly perceived that Robbe-Grillet is drawing the aesthetic consequences from a thoroughgoing atheistic metaphysical conviction, he was thought to be attacking the literature of the past in a gratuitously iconoclastic fashion. 'Far from making a clean sweep of the past,' he points out of himself and his friends in the *nouveau roman*, 'it is on the names of our predecessors that we find it easiest to agree, and our only ambition is to continue where they left off: not to do better, which doesn't make sense, but to follow after them, now, in our day' (*STNN*, p. 137). In other words, he is not saying that the great works of the past are dead, since after all Flaubert wrote the new novel of 1860, and Proust the new novel of 1910, but that to try to write *now* as they wrote *then*, as if Joyce, Kafka and Faulkner had never existed, is an absurdity; worse, it betrays a nostalgia for a time and a metaphysics that are indeed dead and gone, even if the works they threw up live on as the only form of immortality people can hope to know. To indulge in such nostalgia is not only to deceive oneself about the realities of our contemporary situation; it is to commit an act of infidelity towards those very works one claims most to revere, which survive into the present precisely because they were in the vanguard of their own generation, because they were the 'new literature' of their own day.

> The writer must be proud to bear his own date, in the knowledge that there is no masterpiece that exists in eternity, but only works that exist in history, and that they only outlive themselves in so far as they have left the past behind them and heralded the future. (*STNN*, p. 45)

It is clear, then, that, far from being a philistine iconoclast, Robbe-Grillet has a passionate respect for the great writers of the past: 'from Flaubert to Kafka', he says, 'there is a direct line of spiritual descendence, which demands to be continued' (*STNN*, p. 48), and this must lead to a new realism in which there will no longer be the slightest question of 'verisimilitude'. To make his point Robbe-Grillet cites, as so often, the example of Kafka, whose influence on his own work has been all-pervading: Kafka, he says, had the misfortune early on to be saddled with 'profound' meaning by his admirers and exegetists, so that 'when he shows us the offices, the staircases and the corridors where Joseph K. goes in pursuit of justice, it is supposed to be solely to preach the theological notion of "grace" to us' (*STNN*, p. 158). Whereas –

> the one thing we find convincing when we read him with an unprejudiced eye is the absolute reality of the things Kafka describes. The visible world of his novels is certainly, for him, the real world, and what is behind it (if there is anything) seems to be valueless in comparison with the evidence of the objects, actions, words, etc. The hallucinatory effect comes from their extraordinary clarity, and not from any indecision or vagueness. There is no doubt that nothing is more fantastic than precision. Perhaps Kafka's staircases do lead somewhere else, but they are there, you look at them, stair by stair, and follow the details of the banisters. . . . Throughout the work, man's relationship with the world, far from being symbolic, is always direct and immediate. (*STNN*, p. 159)

As is so often the case when one writer discusses the work of a distinguished predecessor – Beckett's early short book on Proust is another case in point – he is meditating upon his own past and future creations as much as he is operating as a literary critic. It is not surprising, therefore, that the above passage tells us as much about how Robbe-Grillet sees his own literary ambition as about Kafka's achievement.[26]

Everything else in Robbe-Grillet follows from these premisses. Once we understand his attitude to our position in the universe, we can see why he is so insistent that literature, and the novel in particular, must eschew what he sees as bankrupt humanism, and develop instead a new realism, a new attitude to time, a new conception of plot, a new approach to character, all of which will be tougher, harder, more transparent than the works of those he sees as 'bankrupt humanists' *par excellence*, Sartre and Camus. His disagreement with Camus stems from his view that he 'tragified' the universe by fostering the notion of the absurd. But the absurd, according to Robbe-Grillet, is 'a form of tragic humanism. It is not a recognition of the separation between man and things. It is a lovers' quarrel, which leads to a crime of passion.' (Robbe-Grillet is here referring to the murder of the Arab by Meursault in *The Outsider*.) 'The world is accused of being an accomplice to murder. . . . Camus does not reject anthropomorphism, he uses it with economy and subtlety, to give it greater weight' (*STNN*, p. 86). An anthropomorphic vocabulary may not in itself appear harmful, but it betrays a whole metaphysical system, a longing for monism. But Robbe-Grillet is a pluralist, and, much as he admires the admirable purity of the opening sentences of *The Outsider*, he cannot forgive Camus for postulating an 'unfathomable abyss that exists between man and the world, between the aspirations of the human spirit and the incapacity of the world to satisfy them' (*STNN*, p. 85). By seeming to exalt humanity, in other words, Camus enslaves it to the absurdity of the Absurd.

With Sartre Robbe-Grillet's quarrel is largely political: he challenges head-on Sartre's prescription that the writer should be politically committed, should actively promote left-wing policies in his works. He sweeps away much Sartrean nonsense with great vigour as simply 'outdated notions'. Certainly, he concedes, the idea of 'a possible union between an artistic rebirth and a politico-economic revolution is one that springs very naturally to mind'; unfortunately, 'the socialist revolution mistrusts revolutionary art, and, what is more, it is not obvious that it is wrong to do so' (*STNN*, pp. 65–6). He points out that, historically speaking, political radicalism and artistic avant-gardism have usually had an uneasy relationship, and that it is sentimental to expect otherwise; sooner or later politicians are going to demand that artists subordinate their art to the revolution and put it at the service of a wider end and an exalted cause. However much artists may themselves believe in that cause, they must inevitably either refuse to serve it – the famous *non serviam* of Stephen Dedalus – or prostitute their talents to it, as a thousand time-serving socialist realists seem happy to do. This is because the true artist 'can only create *for nothing* . . . whatever his attachment to his party or to liberal ideas, at the moment of creation he can only be concerned with the problems of his art' (*STNN*, p. 67).

So, if he rejects Camus's tragic humanism and Sartre's subordination of literature to politics, what role does Robbe-Grillet see for the novel in the latter half of the twentieth century? Like many polemicists, he is clearer about what he is against than what he is for. But it does emerge that he is for a novel that is all 'on the surface', that postulates little or nothing about what may or may not lie behind phenomena; a fiction that presents characters with little or no history, without names or with names that are purely functional (like Jean or Boris, two Robbe-Grillet favourites); a treatment of human time which respects the chronological leaps of the imagination and the temporal distortions of memory or feeling; and a plot that is unashamedly inconsistent, in line with a reality that has its recurring bafflements. Yet he insists that these are not prescriptive statements, but merely indications of a way forward, since each new book 'creates its own rules for itself alone' and the only relation between creation and theoretical reflection on that creation 'is of a dialectical character, a double play of agreement and opposition'; each new work tends after all to 'establish its own functional laws at the same time as it brings about their destruction' (*STNN*, p. 47). So that we have to look at Robbe-Grillet's own practice of fiction in order to find out precisely what innovations he himself has made and so, by implication, recommends to other writers. It was no less a novelist than John Fowles, after all, who said that *Towards a New Novel* was 'indispensable reading for the profession',[27] so in what follows I shall need to refer back occasionally to this main critical statement, with which the novels stand in dialectical relationship (and which incidentally is expertly translated by Barbara Wright).

It might be as well first of all to deal with an objection which was made frequently in France during the early days of Robbe-Grillet's career: that he contradicted himself; that he wrote one thing in his theoretical essays and did another in his novels. I must say that a close reading of both in the light of each other does not bear this out. For instance, it is true that *The Erasers* has a tragic structure and that once the situation is set up the outcome is predictable, just as it is true that *Towards a New Novel* enjoins us to reject 'communion' with things and thus 'reject tragedy' (*STNN*, p. 82), but 'the tragic' means different things in the novel and the essay: in the essay it describes a form of 'unholy complicity' with the world which Robbe-Grillet repudiates, and in the novel it is a matter not of feelings but of shape and purpose. Even where a general note of sadness can be heard, as in the story of the lost soldier of *In the Labyrinth*, this does not amount to the kind of anthropomorphic sentimentality which Robbe-Grillet accuses Camus of peddling, and indeed the last thing one is likely to find in Robbe-Grillet is the cosmic maukishness that existentialism is prone to. In any case the sadness of *In the Labyrinth* is only the other face of the humour of *The House of Assignation* or the ironies of *The Erasers*.

Another inconsistency critics thought they perceived was over the issue of psychology. Robbe-Grillet nowhere states that psychology has no place in fiction, which is perhaps just as well, since, as we have seen, both *Jealousy* and *The Voyeur* are remarkable studies of pathological states of mind, of morbid jealousy and guilty terror respectively. The kind of psychology he is opposed to is the indulgent omniscient variety much honoured by the Goncourt Prize committee, the extended analysis of a character's 'inner' feelings. Robbe-Grillet is too much of a behaviourist – perhaps as a result of his initial scientific training – to have much interest in that sort of thing. Similarly with metaphor: his fiction is densely metaphorical, as for example where the 'black hole' in the centre of Julien's eye in *The Voyeur* is the metaphorical figuration of the 'black hole' into which the text too has swallowed the murder of Jacqueline, and where objects, like the squashed frog in the same book, can represent another object – in this case, for Mathias, the violated body of the young girl. In the film project *Piège à fourrure* Robbe-Grillet openly admits that the sequence of generators he describes amounts to a metaphor of sexual aggression; the image of the labyrinth, too, is omnipresent in his writing. But in none of these instances is the metaphor anthropomorphic: Mathias may project his guilty fantasies on to the squashed frog in the road, but the association implies nothing about the object itself. It is quite different from speaking of a cloud as 'galloping' and using similar 'pananthropic' expressions which 'take the reader out of the universe of forms and plunge him into a universe of meanings' (*STNN*, p. 81).

Certain alleged contradictions having therefore been disposed of, I shall try to state as succinctly as possible what is specifically 'Robbe-Grilletian' about the fictional writing. The underlying principle of unity is the narrator, 'the least neutral and the least impartial of men', always engaged 'in a passionate adventure of the most obsessive type – so obsessive that it often distorts his vision and subjects him to fantasies bordering on delirium' (*STNN*, p. 139). This is undoubtedly the case in *Jealousy*, but in other novels (*The Voyeur*, for example, or *The House of Assignation*) there is another narrative voice, that of the implied author, who intervenes on occasion to comment on the action. Robbe-Grillet does not mention this implied author in his theoretical writings, so far as I am aware, and it is possible that he is not conscious of it as being a separate entity. But its existence bears out his contention that his novels are not 'objective', in the pejorative sense of neutral, cold or impartial, since even where the narrator is not, himself, the obsessed epicentre of the narrative, he is closely involved in the shaping of it: his is the voice, for instance, which welcomes or refuses developments that the text itself generates or seeks to generate, as in *In the Labyrinth, The House of Assignation* or *Project for a Revolution in New York*. He it is, too, who creates suspense as we watch Dupont climbing the stairs for his second and this time fatal encounter with his assassin, Mathias's bicycle breaking down as he hurries already late to the quayside, or Johnson rushing into the police ambush in the Villa Bleue. It is he who, Chandler-like, leaves some things unexplained, such as why Jean Robin seems to be still alive while long dead in *The Voyeur*; he is directly responsible for the fact that 'it isn't events that are lacking, it is only their character of certainty, their tranquillity and their innocence' (*STNN*, p. 64).

Turning now from the narrator to the plot, I pointed out in a previous chapter that the early novels in particular do have a basic story-line which tempers uncertainty about what is happening. In any case the text has a reassuring habit of returning to previous scenes and filling them out, so that the attentive reader cannot really get lost. As Robbe-Grillet agrees, '*The Erasers* and *The Voyeur* do both contain a "plot" of the most easily discernible kind, and, what's more, they abound in elements which are usually considered dramatic' (*STNN*, p. 64). The fact that he keeps the reader guessing about the murder in *The Erasers*, or the rape in *The Voyeur*, does not in itself make him a more 'difficult' novelist than, say, Graham Greene or John le Carré, who do the same thing; Greene in particular can be a very opaque writer for anyone not familiar with his oblique methods of narration. Moreover, Robbe-Grillet was willing, at least up to about 1963, to give his works a clear, firm, broadly linear structure. *The Erasers*, for instance, returns to its point of departure, and the structure of *Marienbad* and *La Japonaise* is similarly circular. *Jealousy* and *In the Labyrinth* have a kind of rise and fall, a sort of ballistic curve. *The Voyeur* is divided into three equal parts, corresponding broadly to the period leading up to Jacqueline's rape, the hours preceding the failure to catch the boat, and the time between then and Mathias's actual departure; here, as in *The Erasers*, Robbe-Grillet pays close attention to chapterization, and gives it an organizational as well as a structuring function. *The Immortal One* has a double ending, the second closely mirroring the first and serving to underline strongly the parallel with the Orpheus and Eurydice legend (in that N/Orpheus loses, finds and loses again, this time for good, L/Eurydice, and so can only join her in death).

From the mid-sixties on there is a change, in that Robbe-Grillet abandons linear plots and becomes much more interested in *générateurs* or textual triggers, in fictions-within-fictions, and in sudden shifts in the narrative which result from different textual associations. Nevertheless, although the application of these devices becomes more far-reaching in the last two decades, they were not invented in *The House of Assignation*: the text jumps back in time through association in *The Erasers*, for instance, and Mathias is found telling the story of his day to islanders in a fairly accurate manner, leaving out only the detour he made to look for Jacqueline on the cliffs. Why Robbe-Grillet changed course in the mid-sixties is an interesting speculation. He may have been influenced by film technique through firsthand acquaintance with the way a film is made – that is, in pieces which are then put together in the cutting-room; he was probably also affected by the 'explanations' given of his working methods by such neo-formalist critics in France as Jean Ricardou – that is, he may unconsciously have been led to create texts in the mechanistic way they said he did. Probably both explanations can be accepted. It is certainly arguable that Robbe-Grillet has suffered more, as an artist, from the adulation of radical critics of the *Tel Quel* school than ever he did from the hostility of traditional critics at the start of his career. It seems to have led him to think that he could indulge his sado-erotic fantasies openly and respectably by the convenient device of calling these impulses 'generators', but he was also assisted by the relaxation of moral censorship in France after 1968.

As for film, Robbe-Grillet has always been fascinated by 'its subjective and imaginative possibilities' (*STNN*, p. 146). He certainly has made the most of them himself, especially the highly suggestive juxtaposition of different sound and image. It is, of course, a familiar convention of the cinema that the sound-track can carry a different part of the narrative from that actually appearing on the screen (the hero's car can be seen driving away while the heroine is still heard sobbing over his departure, for example). But Robbe-Grillet takes the practice much further than usual, and so is able in *The Immortal One*, for instance, to play music on the sound-track which evokes a mood relevant to a quite different time from that shown on the screen. He also exploits the possibility which the film shares with a musical score, that of being able to make frequent reprises and repeats with variations. And last but not least he has been able in recent years to achieve strongly erotic effects by filming the most beautiful girls that money can hire in provocative situations and poses; the special issue of *Obliques* reproduces some memorable stills of Catherine Jourdan in the nude, for instance, taken from *L'Eden et après*. It has to be said, however, that when such actresses are not in frame there is a considerable visual monotony about Robbe-Grillet's films: he is far from having the same talent with the viewfinder as he has with words.

His prose style, after all, is what will ensure his survival. It is at once inimitable and instantly recognizable: formal, impersonal, literary but also elegant and direct. His descriptions of familiar things have something of the immediacy and concreteness of Flaubert's, and the hallucinatory intensity of Kafka's. He uses free indirect speech with the accomplished ease of a master. And even when his subject-matter is repellent he writes prose of great sonority and clarity. He takes as much trouble over the balance of his sentences as Flaubert ever did. Whatever later generations think of his works as fiction, he will be remembered as one of the great stylists in the French language. Here he is at his most characteristic:

> It is no rare occurrence, in fact, in a modern novel, to find a description that starts from nothing. It doesn't begin by giving the reader a general picture, it seems to spring from a minute and unimportant detail, which is more like a geometrical point than anything else – a starting point – from which it invents lines, planes, and a whole architecture, and our impression that these are being invented in the course of the description is reinforced by the fact that it suddenly contradicts itself, repeats itself, thinks better of it, branches off in a different direction, etc. The reader is beginning to get a glimpse of something, though, and thinks that this something is going to be made clearer. But the lines of the drawing go on accumulating, and it becomes overloaded; they con-

tradict each other, and change places until the very construction of the image renders it more and more uncertain. A few more paragraphs, and when the description is complete, you discover that it hasn't left anything permanent behind it: in the end, it has become a twofold movement of getting created and getting stuck, and this ambiguity you also find in the book on every level, and more particularly in the sum total of its structure, and this is where the *disappointment* inherent in the writing of today originates. (*STNN*, pp. 145–6)

It is a pity, one is tempted to think at this point, that one is not disappointed in this way more often.

Robbe-Grillet's rigour has found a distinguished champion in Susan Sontag. She praises his 'complex criticism of the notions of tragedy and of humanism, the unremitting clarity with which he demolishes the old shibboleth of form versus content' and 'the compatibility of his aesthetic with technical innovations in the novel quite different from those he has chosen'; she goes on to say that 'Robbe-Grillet's essays are truly radical and, if one grants but a single of his assumptions, carry one all the way to conviction.' This endorsement from across the Atlantic must have pleased him, since Susan Sontag, unlike some of his supporters in Paris, has no personal axe to grind but simply states things as they are. It is particularly noteworthy that she says his theory has other openings than the novels he or his disciples like Ricardou or Philippe Sollers have written, and one can indeed envisage ways of writing fiction – such as those of the younger British writers like Ian McEwan or Adam Mars-Jones – which are radically different from Robbe-Grillet's but which derive their justification in part from his demolition job on the comforting metaphysics that underpin attempts to write now as if nothing has changed since the days of the Barchester Chronicles. As Susan Sontag pertinently points out, 'the novel as a form of art has nothing to lose, and everything to gain, by joining the revolution that has already swept over most of the other arts.'[28] The standard-bearer of that revolution, whether we like it or not, is Alain Robbe-Grillet.

It is true that Sontag – who wrote that essay two decades ago – is now anti-formalist, but her endorsement has since been taken up more widely within the United States. The experimental novelist John Hawkes has gone so far as to claim, for example, that the true enemies of the novel are plot, character, setting and theme, and that something that he calls 'totality of vision or structure' is all that remains.[29] In the pictorial arts and in the theatre there has been a growing tendency to resist metaphor, to go for texture and immediacy, to cling to surface and to downgrade meaning. Ralph Goings, for instance, has

> actually acknowledged Robbe-Grillet's *The Voyeur* as a factor in his own development towards photorealism, recalling in particular that moment in which the protagonist, remembering the sight of a seagull on a window ledge, realizes that he can recall nothing of the emotional overtones of the moment but only the physical details of feathers, colour and texture.[30]

Inside France, too, Robbe-Grillet has already achieved something positive. He has often attacked Sartre, as we have seen, for what he calls the dishonesty of his attitude to art. This consists, Robbe-Grillet argues, of denigrating literature and exalting instead 'useful' activities like science and engineering. Robbe-Grillet, as an applied scientist himself, is well placed to know that science is for the most part speculative, and researchers often have scant idea of, and perhaps little interest in, any practical outcome from their experiments. He tells the story of a great scientist who spent a not inconsiderable part of his time dropping a piece of string on the ground in order to make a statistical study of the shape it adopted as it fell.[31] Is that, Robbe-Grillet wonders, any more 'down to earth' than writing novels which are lucky if they sell initially 1500 copies?

Another disinterested Anglo-Saxon observer, John Cruickshank, in an article significantly entitled 'Limitations of the

Intellectual', noted that Sartre and Simone de Beauvoir 'had registered the collapse of the commitment dream by 1960'. The date is important, since it was around that time that Robbe-Grillet's ideas – and particularly his insistence that the writer as writer (as opposed, of course, to the private citizen) has no business trying to influence political developments – were starting to have an impact. According to Cruickshank, Simone de Beauvoir admitted to Madeleine Chapsal, a leading French literary journalist, that 'a writer never engages in political work as a writer', while Sartre told the same interviewer that 'he had lost the illusion that literature can bring about political change'.[32] This was just as well, since, while his importance in the history of ideas can hardly be exaggerated, Sartre's influence on actual political developments was negligible.

All Robbe-Grillet is asking for is honesty about this. His own political position is quite radical, and he has not been afraid to stand up for his ideas when the occasion demanded it – as, for instance, when he signed the famous 'Declaration of the 121' about the duty of military insubordination when the French army was fighting the FLN in Algeria. But he never puts his creative writings to political purposes, simply because he is well aware that this would destroy them and that it would be totally ineffective. In France in the 1950s it badly needed someone to put the cat among the pigeons by spelling this out.

6

CONCLUSION

Things are never definitively in order. (*The House of Assignation*)

As I have frequently implied, Robbe-Grillet is a lover of the paradox, and so it is perhaps fitting that the concluding remarks of a study of his work should to some extent go counter to the general tenor of what has been said up till now. Like Robbe-Grillet, I do not see that as contradiction but as healthy dialectic.

I want now to suggest that modernism – that great literary and artistic movement which began around the 1890s and continued vigorously on and off for several decades, at least until the early 1970s – is now in a terminal decline, and that (not perhaps so very surprisingly) Robbe-Grillet has helped willy-nilly to bring about its final demise while claiming to revitalize it. He represents in his first phase – what one might call his 'labyrinthine' period – the culmination of a certain tendency in modernism, which begins, so far as the novel is concerned, with Flaubert and attains its highest point in Kafka, whose influence on Robbe-Grillet is, as we have seen, immense. It is a tendency which reaches a particular and self-inflicted dead end in Samuel Beckett's fiction. In his first phase Robbe-Grillet undertook, as Marxists might say, almost single-handedly the objective analysis of the situation with which Kafka and Beckett left the novelist. He wrote his immensely influential essays – and, at least at first, somewhat less influential novels – as a direct outcome of this analysis. For some time I believed this analysis to be broadly correct and I argued the point in such books as *New Directions in Literature* (1968) and *Claude Simon and Fiction Now* (1975). But I now incline to think it is wrong, or at least only partially correct. Even if it is wrong, however, this does not make Robbe-Grillet any less significant as a contemporary writer and thinker: quite the contrary.

There are now, it seems to me, unmistakable signs that the particular post-modernism that Robbe-Grillet so typically and centrally represents is dead, and that his efforts to find 'a path for the future novel' (the title of one of his essays) have paradoxically but no doubt understandably condemned to oblivion some of the novels he wrote in his first phase, together with a number of others written by less gifted and more dogmatic disciples. One can, like Susan Sontag, accept the premises from which Robbe-Grillet derives his theory of a new realism, and even applaud the ananthropomorphic re-vision of humanity's relations with the universe which he so convincingly argues for, and still find that his novels fail in so far as they derive too directly from that theory. Fortunately some of the early novels – *The Voyeur*, *Jealousy* and *In the Labyrinth*, in particular – transcend the dogma and remain impressive in their own right as fictions, eruptions from the unconscious which subvert the conscious constructions of thought. Indeed, Robbe-Grillet would probably not dissent from this, since he stresses that his essays derive from a different source than the fiction. With the passage of time, it is clear which of the 'labyrinthine' novels succeed as works of art and which do not. *Un Régicide* is an interesting piece of juvenilia, *The Erasers* is a clever puzzle, *The Voyeur* and *Jealousy* powerfully chart the meanderings of the sick mind, and *In the Labyrinth* is a moving novel of suffering and loss. But what is now obvious about the last three is that they succeed in spite of, rather than because of, the doctrine of a new realism.

Around the early 1960s Robbe-Grillet seems himself to have sensed that this type of fiction was finished. There is a gap of some six years between the publication of *In the Labyrinth*, the last novel of the first phase, and *The House of Assignation*, the first work of what now appears clearly as a second phase. During the interval Robbe-Grillet turned his attention to the cinema, and when he returned to the novel he struck a new note: that of a particularly sadistic form of eroticism, which has continued up to the present time. There were, of course, erotic themes earlier, especially in *The Voyeur*, but they were subordinated to the pursuit of the new realism.

I have already said that *The House of Assignation* is a witty and charming book, and that *Project for a Revolution in New York* is an interesting treatment of the inexhaustibly fascinating (to Europeans especially) myth of the American Dream. But the remaining novels and films of his second phase are mechanical and disappointing, even if one is not put off, as I am, by the increasingly repulsive subject-matter. It is one thing to explore the mind of a man who derives satisfaction from torturing a young girl with burning cigarette ends, as is the case with *The Voyeur*, and quite another to present such obscenities as if they were fantasies we all indulge in, which is what Robbe-Grillet asserts in later works.

Meanwhile, as I have said, the other major talents of the *nouveau roman* have gone their separate ways, exploring and developing new forms of realism such as Robbe-Grillet advocated in general terms in the 1950s but soon became incapable of creating for himself. Claude Simon, for instance, has at the age of nearly 70 produced a rich and dense novel, *The Georgics*, which is probably his masterpiece. And younger French writers of notable gifts, such as Tony Duvert, have sought to create poetic fictions which owe much to Robbe-Grillet's early works and his courageous attacks on the anthropomorphic sentimentality of his predecessors. The depressing thing is that Duvert is now developing independently a line in poetic realism which has more in common with the innovations of younger British writers, like Ian McEwan, while Robbe-Grillet has been left behind in the sado-erotic gothicism of J. G. Ballard, a novelist who also, in his early books, showed much promise.

Nevertheless, even if his achievement as a novelist and film-maker is uneven, and if his more recent theoretical pronouncements (especially about the innocuity of pornography) are often silly, Robbe-Grillet is a person of remarkable intellectual distinction who stands head and shoulders above most other members of the Paris intelligentsia. He will turn out to have had an importance in French literary and intellectual history in this century comparable only to Sartre's. In fact, although he opposed Sartre on almost every point, he is not unlike him: both men are probably intellectuals first and creative writers second, and both are the products of a particularly French form of rigorous mental training, Sartre in philosophy at the Ecole Normale Supérieure and Robbe-Grillet in natural sciences at the Institut National Agronomique. As a result, both have, or in Sartre's case had, minds as incisive as any of their generation. And like Sartre Robbe-Grillet is a critic in the broadest sense of the term: someone who, on the British scene, would be a combination of A. J. Ayer, Frank Kermode and Harold Pinter rolled into one. As for his position within the *nouveau roman*, I think posterity's verdict will be that he is its André Breton, and Claude Simon its Paul Eluard: that is, Robbe-Grillet is the brilliant publicist and theorist of the tendency and Simon is its great poet-novelist. Robbe-Grillet remains by far the best-known 'new novelist' in Britain and the United States, an immensely articulate exponent of a certain kind of post-modernism which may now be moribund but which is central to the literary history of France since the war. His very unevenness and paradoxes, in particular his change in direction in the middle of his career, are themselves profoundly characteristic not only of the writer himself but of the whole contemporary literary scene.

And this in spite of the fact that he has become in recent years something of a guru, an attender of literary gatherings of the most sycophantic kind. In his early career he had virtually the whole of the French literary establishment against him; now he is a leading member of that establishment himself. Unfortunately there is no young Robbe-Grillet in the offing to challenge *him*; even past 60 he is still, for better or for worse, the avant-garde. His creative writings have become more stereotyped and his theoretical pronouncements more arcane. He is no longer a revitalizing force in contemporary French literature – if anything, a deadening one. He is largely to blame for the manneristic academicism which now dominates literary magazines in France, even if he does not greatly approve of it; and although he does not aspire to Breton's eminence, being a much more liberal and more tolerant man, he travels to too many meetings of academic critics and esoteric writers where he is expected willy-nilly to hold court. It is easy, therefore, to see him as a spent force in an exhausted literary milieu.

This would, however, be to write him off too soon. He published a superb short text in 1978, the *Fragment autobiographique imaginaire*, a section of his contribution to the well-known 'Par lui-même' series of literary biographies which still has not appeared as this study goes to press. This piece shows that he can write as sensitively, wittily and intelligently as ever in a prose of crystalline clarity. The complete 'Par lui-même' volume, if and when it comes out, will certainly show that Robbe-Grillet is still a figure to be reckoned with in the literature of our time.

NOTES

1 John Fowles, *The French Lieutenant's Woman* (St Albans: Panther, 1970), p. 85.
2 See John Sturrock, 'The Project of A l'aine robe grillée', *Twentieth-Century Studies*, 6 (1971), p. 16; and *Project for a Revolution in New York*, p. 65.
3 *Fragment autobiographique imaginaire*, p. 6.
4 *Robbe-Grillet: analyse, théorie*, ed. Jean Ricardou (Paris: Union Générale d'Editions, 1976), vol. 2, p. 418.
5 Roger Poole, 'Objectivity and Subjectivity in the Nouveau Roman', *Twentieth-Century Studies*, 6 (1971), p. 73.
6 Ann Jefferson, *The Nouveau Roman and the Poetics of Fiction* (Cambridge: Cambridge University Press, 1980), p. 209.
7 Samuel Beckett, *Watt* (Paris: Olympia Press, 1953), p. 74.
8 Phillip Simpson, 'The Only Morality is Information', *The Listener*, 16 September 1982, p. 32.
9 Derek Robinson, 'The Plot Curdles', BBC Radio 3, 24 January 1983.
10 Gabriele Annan, 'Raymond Chandler's Epigrams', *The Listener*, 31 December 1981, p. 823.
11 R.S., 'Et si Chandler n'était qu'une poignée de tics?', *Le Monde*, 11 May 1979, p. 19.
12 Quoted in *La Jalousie*, ed. B. G. Garnham (London: Methuen Educational, 1969), p. xiv.
13 See Jefferson, op. cit., p. 30.
14 *Minuit*, 18 (March 1976), p. 2.
15 Henry Tube (pseud. of John Spurling), 'To the Barricades!', *The Spectator*, 16 February 1968, p. 201.
16 *La Jalousie*, ed. Garnham, p. xxv.
17 Pierre Schneider, 'Gustave Moreau, roi de la nuit', *L'Express*, 22 June 1961.

18 A characteristic Robbe-Grillet stylistic 'thumbprint' is the use of *soi*, where standard syntax would give *lui*, in phrases like *devant soi*.

19 *The Collected Essays, Journalism and Letters of George Orwell*, ed. Sonia Orwell and Ian Angus (Harmondsworth: Penguin, 1970), vol. 3, p. 260.

20 Roy Armes, *The Films of Alain Robbe-Grillet* (Amsterdam: John Benjamins, 1981), pp. 159–60.

21 Many popular novels, films and plays project this image of Hong Kong. A recent example was the radio play *The Last Cargo of the Cathay Queen* by Philip Latham, broadcast on BBC Radio 4 on 17 February 1983.

22 *The Times* (London), 21 August 1982, p. 4.

23 *Le Monde*, 30 October 1970, p. 18.

24 See chapter 7, 'Images and Promises in the Western Sky', in my book *Novel and Reader* (London: Marion Boyars, 1980).

25 Martin Seymour-Smith, *Who's Who in Twentieth-Century Literature* (London: Weidenfeld & Nicolson, 1976), p. 313; Frank Kermode, 'Modernisms', in Bernard Bergonzi (ed.), *Innovations* (London: Macmillan, 1968), p. 76 *n*.

26 The Paris literary monthly *Critique* announced in its April 1960 issue that a future number would contain an article by Robbe-Grillet entitled 'Kafka réaliste'. Although the essay unfortunately never appeared, it would probably have developed at greater length Robbe-Grillet's view, expressed elsewhere, that Kafka is a realist writer first and foremost, and would no doubt have stressed such instances of this as the detailed description of Joseph K's daily round in *The Trial*.

27 John Fowles, 'Notes on an Unfinished Novel', in Thomas McCormack (ed.), *Afterwords: Novelists on their Novels* (New York: Harper & Row, 1969), p. 165.

28 Susan Sontag, *Against Interpretation and Other Essays* (New York: Noonday Press, 1966), p. 111.

29 Quoted in Malcolm Bradbury (ed.), *The Novel Today* (London: Fontana, 1977), p. 7.

30 Quoted by Christopher Bigsby in *A Critical Introduction to Twentieth-Century American Drama*, vol. 3 (Cambridge: Cambridge University Press, forthcoming).

31 Interview in *L'Express*, 1–7 April 1968, p. 42.

32 *The Times Higher Education Supplement*, 26 February 1982, p. 14.

BIBLIOGRAPHY

WORKS BY ALAIN ROBBE-GRILLET

Novels

Les Gommes. Paris: Editions de Minuit, 1953. Trans. Richard Howard as *The Erasers*. New York: Grove Press, 1964. London: Calder & Boyars, 1966.

Le Voyeur. Paris: Editions de Minuit, 1955. Trans. Richard Howard as *The Voyeur*. New York: Grove Press, 1958. London: John Calder, 1959.

La Jalousie. Paris: Editions de Minuit, 1957. Trans. Richard Howard as *Jealousy*. New York: Grove Press, 1959. London: John Calder, 1960.

Dans le labyrinthe. Paris: Editions de Minuit, 1959. Trans. Richard Howard as *In the Labyrinth*. New York: Grove Press, 1960. Trans. Christine Brooke-Rose as *In the Labyrinth* (the trans. used in this study). London: Calder & Boyars, 1967.

La Maison de rendez-vous. Paris: Editions de Minuit, 1965. Trans. Richard Howard as *La Maison de Rendez-Vous*. New York: Grove Press, 1966. Trans. A. M. Sheridan Smith as *The House of Assignation* (the trans. used in this study). London: Calder & Boyars, 1970.

Projet pour une révolution à New York. Paris: Editions de Minuit, 1970. Trans. Richard Howard as *Project for a Revolution in New York*. New York: Grove Press, 1972. London: Calder & Boyars, 1973.

Topologie d'une cité fantôme. Paris: Editions de Minuit, 1976. Trans. J. A. Underwood as *Topology of a Phantom City*. New York: Grove Press, 1977. London: John Calder, 1978.

Un Régicide (written in 1949). Paris: Editions de Minuit, 1978.

Souvenirs du triangle d'or. Paris: Editions de Minuit, 1978.

Short fiction

Instantanés. Paris: Editions de Minuit, 1962. Trans. Bruce Morrissette as *Snapshots*. New York: Grove Press, 1968. Trans. Barbara Wright as *Snapshots* (the trans. used in this study), in *Snapshots and Towards a New Novel*. London: Calder & Boyars, 1965.

Cine-novels

L'Année dernière à Marienbad. Paris: Editions de Minuit, 1961. Trans. Richard Howard as *Last Year at Marienbad*. New York: Grove Press, 1962. London: John Calder, 1962.

L'Immortelle. Paris: Editions de Minuit, 1963. Trans. A. M. Sheridan Smith as *The Immortal One*. London: Calder & Boyars, 1971.

Glissements progressifs du plaisir. Paris: Editions de Minuit, 1974.

Criticism and literary theory

Pour un nouveau roman. Paris: Editions de Minuit, 1963. Trans. Richard Howard as *For a New Novel*. New York: Grove Press, 1966. Trans. Barbara Wright as *Towards a New Novel* (the trans. used in this study), in *Snapshots and Towards a New Novel*. London: Calder & Boyars, 1965.

Miscellaneous (excluding early scientific publications)

L'Image (by 'Jean de Berg'). Paris: Editions de Minuit, 1956.

Rêves de jeunes filles. (Text by Robbe-Grillet, later collected in *Topologie d'une cité fantôme*; photographs by David Hamilton.) Paris: Robert Laffont, 1971. Trans. Elizabeth Walter as *Dreams of a Young Girl*. New York: Morrow, 1971. Same trans. as *Dreams of Young Girls*. London: Collins, 1971.

Les Demoiselles d'Hamilton. (Text by Robbe-Grillet, later collected in *Topologie d'une cité fantôme*; photographs by David Hamilton.) Paris: Robert Laffont, 1972. Trans. Martha Egan as *Sisters*. New York: Morrow, 1973. London: Collins, 1976.

La Belle Captive. (Text by Robbe-Grillet, later collected in *Topologie d'une cité fantôme* and in *Souvenirs du triangle d'or*; illustrations by René Magritte.) Lausanne: Bibliothèque des Arts, 1975.

Construction d'un temple en ruines à la déesse Vanadé. (Text by Robbe-Grillet, later collected in *Topologie d'une cité fantôme*; etchings by Paul Delvaux.) Paris: Le Bateau-Lavoir, 1975. Limited edition.

Temple aux miroirs. (Text by Robbe-Grillet, later collected in *Souvenirs du triangle d'or*; photographs by Irina Ionesco.) Paris: Seghers, 1977.

Fragment autobiographique imaginaire. (Extract from *Alain Robbe-Grillet par lui-même.* Paris: Seuil, forthcoming.) *Minuit*, 31 (November 1978), pp. 2–8.

Obliques, 16–17 (1978), pp. 1–284. (Robbe-Grillet special issue; contains many previously unpublished or uncollected minor texts.)

Traces suspectes en surface. (Text by Robbe-Grillet, reprinted from *Topologie d'une cité fantôme*; lithographs by Robert Rauschenberg.) New York: Tatyana Grosman, 1979. Limited edition.

Le Rendez-vous. (French text by Robbe-Grillet, a complete version of which was later published in *Djinn*; exercises, vocabulary, etc., by Yvone Lenard.) New York: CBS College Publishing, 1981.

Djinn: un trou rouge entre les pavés disjoints. Paris: Editions de Minuit, 1981. Trans. Yvone Lenard and Walter Wells as *Djinn*. New York: Grove Press, 1982. London: John Calder, 1983.

Chausse-trappes. ('Roman-photo' by Edward Lachman and Elieba Levine; preface by Robbe-Grillet.) Paris: Editions de Minuit, 1981.

Films (directed by Robbe-Grillet except where otherwise stated)

L'Année dernière à Marienbad (*Last Year at Marienbad*). 1961. Script and dialogue by Robbe-Grillet, directed by Alain Resnais.

L'Immortelle (*The Immortal One*). 1963.

Trans-Europ-Express. 1966.

L'Homme qui ment. 1968.

L'Eden et après. 1970.

N a pris les dés. 1971.

Glissements progressifs du plaisir. 1974.

Le Jeu avec le feu. 1975.

La Belle Captive. 1983.

BIBLIOGRAPHY

Useful bibliographies are contained in the *Obliques* special issue (see above) and in Roy Armes's book (see below). For secondary material up to 1972, see also Dale Watson Fraizer, *Alain Robbe-Grillet: An Annotated Bibliography of Critical Studies 1953–1972* (Metuchen, NJ: Scarecrow Press, 1973).

SELECTED CRITICISM ON ROBBE-GRILLET
AND THE *NOUVEAU ROMAN*

Armes, Roy. *The Films of Alain Robbe-Grillet.* Amsterdam: John Benjamins, 1981.

Barthes, Roland. *Essais critiques.* Paris: Editions du Seuil, 1964.

Fletcher, John. *New Directions in Literature.* London: Calder & Boyars, 1968.

——. *Claude Simon and Fiction Now.* London: Calder & Boyars, 1975.

Heath, Stephen. *The Nouveau Roman: A Study in the Practice of Writing.* London: Elek, 1972.

Janvier, Ludovic. *Une Parole exigeante: le nouveau roman.* Paris: Editions de Minuit, 1964.

Jefferson, Ann. *The Nouveau Roman and the Poetics of Fiction.* Cambridge: Cambridge University Press, 1980.

Morrissette, Bruce. *Les Romans de Robbe-Grillet.* Paris: Editions de Minuit, 1963. Trans. and revised by the author as *The Novels of Robbe-Grillet.* Ithaca, NY: Cornell University Press, 1975.

Ricardou, Jean. *Pour une théorie du nouveau roman.* Paris: Editions du Seuil, 1971.

—— (ed.). *Robbe-Grillet: analyse, théorie.* 2 vols. Paris: Union Générale d'Editions, 1976.

Roudiez, Leon S. *French Fiction Today: A New Direction.* New Brunswick, NJ: Rutgers University Press, 1972.

Sturrock, John. *The French New Novel.* London: Oxford University Press, 1969.